E

MASTERS
OF CRIME

MASTERS OF CRIME

FICTION'S FINEST VILLAINS
AND THEIR
REAL-LIFE INSPIRATIONS

ADAM NIGHTINGALE

The History Press

To Simon Hammond. '*I shot him six times.*'

'I knew not what wild beast we were about to hunt down in the dark jungle of criminal London, but I was well assured, from the bearing of this master huntsman, that the adventure was a most grave one ...'

The Empty House, Arthur Conan Doyle

LEICESTER LIBRARIES	
Askews & Holts	31-Aug-2011
	£18.99

First published 2011

The History Press
The Mill, Brimscombe Port
Stroud, Gloucestershire, GL5 2QG
www.thehistorypress.co.uk

© Adam Nightingale 2011

The right of Adam Nightingale to be identified as the Author of this work has been asserted in accordance with the Copyrights, Designs and Patents Act 1988.

British Library Cataloguing in Publication Data.
A catalogue record for this book is available from the British Library.

ISBN 978 0 7524 5418 4

Typesetting and origination by The History Press
Printed in Great Britain

CONTENTS

Acknowledgements

Thanks to Pete Nightingale, Susannah Nightingale, Alec and Jo Cobb, Matt and Louise Frost, Gio Baffa, Pollie Shorthouse, Bev Baker, the staff of the Galleries of Justice Museum of Crime and Punishment, Paul Baker, Maureen from Towncentric – Gravesend Tourist Information Centre, Micah Harris and Max Allen Collins.

PART ONE:

THE BUILDING BLOCKS OF MASTER VILLAINY

1

THE GREAT FEUD

'Have you read of Jonathan Wild?'
'Well, the name has a familiar sound. Someone in a novel, was he not?
I don't take much stock of detectives in novels — chaps that do things and
never let you see them do them. That's just inspiration, not business.'
'Jonathan Wild wasn't in a novel. He was a master criminal and he lived last
century.'
'Then he's no use to me. I'm a practical man.'

The Valley of Fear, Arthur Conan Doyle

WILD

On 31 March 1716, mother and son John and Mary Knapp were attacked by
a gang of five men whilst returning from an evening at Sadler's Wells. John
Knapp was knocked to the ground and the thieves took his hat and wig. Mary
Knapp shouted for help. One of the gang members produced a pistol and shot
her dead. A reward was immediately posted for the attackers' capture.

The gang comprised Thomas Thurland, John Chapman, Timothy Dun,
Isaac Rag and William White (the murderer). On 8 April, barely a week after
the crime had been committed, William White was drinking and whoring at
the home of a friend in Newtoners Lane. Two men arrived at the house. One
was short and wiry and spoke with a West Midlands accent; the other was a
Jew. The two men subdued White and took him to the Roundhouse to be
locked up. The West Midlander was Jonathan Wild, the self-proclaimed Thief
Taker General of Great Britain and Ireland. His companion was Abraham
Mendez, Wild's tough and loyal sergeant-at-arms and first among equals of

Abraham Mendez shoots Timothy Dun while he is trying to escape. (Illustrated by Stephen Dennis)

the many self-styled law enforcers at the Thief Taker General's beck and call. Soon after, Thurland and Chapman joined White on the gallows. Isaac Rag was captured but spared Tyburn and put in the pillory instead after informing on twenty-two of his fellow thieves. All four men had been hunted down by Wild and his associates in a very short space of time. Only Timothy Dun was still at large.

Dun had gone into hiding. Wild was confident that given a little time Dun would surface and give himself away. He had even placed a bet of 10 guineas that he would have Dun in custody before the next court sessions. Dun, for his part, was wondering whether in fact the impetus to catch him had subsided. Most of the gang had been caught and, more importantly, the murderer had been executed. Dun sent his wife to approach Wild personally and test the water as to the exact nature of his current fugitive status. It was a bold move and risky on Dun's part, but his wife was cautious and took extra care to make sure that none of Wild's men tried to follow her. She took an elaborate route back to her husband, criss-crossing the Thames and finally ending up in Lambeth, before she was confident that she had done enough to shake off any tracker Wild may have dispatched to tail her. She then returned to Dun's hideout in Southwark.

Wild's men were much more skilful than Dun's wife had anticipated. She had been successfully followed and her house had been marked with chalk. Wild arrived in the morning with Abraham Mendez, a Mr Riddleson and an unnamed man. Dun heard Wild approach and he tried to make his escape out of the back window, two floors above street level and 8ft from the ground. Mendez spotted him and shot him in the arm, causing Dun to fall to the ground. Riddleson then shot him in the face. Dun survived his two gunshot wounds, but was subsequently tried and hanged.

A violent and murderous gang had been permanently broken up by the industry and courage of Jonathan Wild and his small army of amateur law enforcers. Wild hadn't done it for free. The rewards posted for the gang's capture would have been substantial, but in an extremely violent city, where official methods of policing were woefully unequal to the task, Wild's name was synonymous to many with justice. By 1725, Wild could boast of having been responsible for hanging in excess of sixty criminals. He had twice had his skull fractured, had received numerous wounds and wore an ugly scar where his throat had been slashed – all physical tokens of his devotion to civil order. But others knew better. In actuality, Wild's activities were a highly mercenary and sophisticated smokescreen masking a vast criminal empire that regulated the movements and activities of virtually every criminal in London. Wild was the first English crime baron. His exploits, when finally exposed, would scandalise his peers and provide the archetypal example for satirists,

Under the guise of the Thief Taker General of Great Britain and Ireland, Jonathan Wild
hunted down any criminal that refused to do business with him. (*The Chronicles of Crime*, Vol. I,
T. Miles & Co., 1891)

novelists, playwrights, journalists and crime writers to draw on for genera-
tions to come.

Jonathan Wild was born in Wolverhampton around 1683, although the
exact date of his birth is not known. His father was either a wig-maker or a
carpenter whilst his mother was a market trader. For his class and social station, Jonathan Wild was well educated. By the age of 15 he could read, write,
was numerate and had been apprenticed to a buckle-maker. By 19 he had

married and by 20 he had fathered a son. A year later he had abandoned them both and travelled to London.

The London of the early eighteenth century was vicious, overcrowded, squalid, wealthy and tantalising. The chasm between luxury and poverty was enormous. The systems of law enforcement that relied on constables and nightwatchmen to patrol a London divided and subdivided by archaic parish borders was swamped by the sudden and massive surge in the population. London arguably became the most lawless it had ever been in its entire history. It was a deeply licentious place and irresistible to Jonathan Wild.

Wild worked at being a buckle-maker only for a short period of time. His lifestyle was profligate and his earnings couldn't keep pace with his appetites. He was arrested for debt and thrown into the Wood Street Compter, where he served four years. Imprisonment was difficult for Wild. Wood Street was split into two sides: one relatively comfortable; the other harsh and disgusting. Where you were placed was entirely dependent on what you could afford to pay the authorities. Jonathan Wild had no money and no friends willing or rich enough to subsidise him. Lack of funds therefore consigned him to the Common Side of the Compter and Wild was forced to fend for himself.

Yet Wild survived. In time he won the confidence of the gaoler and he was given a job helping the gaoler to manage prisoners brought in during the night, ferrying them back and forth between the Justices of the Peace and the Compter. In this capacity, Wild met Mary Miliner. As one of the most notorious pickpockets and prostitutes of the era, Miliner was shrewd, tough and well connected. She would become the first of two mentors that schooled Wild thoroughly in the workings of the London underworld. He would outgrow both of them, assimilating and superseding anything that they could teach him, leaving one of them permanently disfigured and the other a ruin. All of that was to come, but for the time being Wild was the perfect student. Miliner paid off his debt and he went to work for her.

Initially, Wild and Miliner got on very well. They became lovers and lived together as man and wife. Wild worked as Miliner's 'Twang', Georgian slang for a prostitute's thug, bodyguard, protector or pimp. But the word pimp in this context is misleading; Miliner was the boss and Wild's principal function was as a participant in a humiliating and brutal form of theft. Miliner would pick up a client, have sex with him, while Wild robbed him at his most distracted and vulnerable.

Wild was a consummate observer. In Wood Street he had watched and learned how a certain level of the thieving classes operated, mentally processing the information and secretly devising ways in which their various methodologies could be refined and improved. Under Mary Miliner a whole new strata of criminal life was open to him. Mary introduced Wild to much of the city's criminal royalty. Wild got to know the capital's divers gangs, their operations and their hideouts. He realised very quickly that intelligence was artillery and stored the information away for a time when it might come in handy.

In the meantime, Wild and Miliner prospered. They established a brothel and bought an alehouse in Cripplegate that also doubled as a brothel. Wild had something of a genius for nefarious administration and would organise and direct the gangs of thieves affiliated with Milliner, sending them out to steal and co-ordinating their actions, making a point of never personally going with them or directly participating in a crime. He was extremely good at what he did. The gangs greatly respected his powers of organisation and Wild and Miliner made even more money, but Wild was beginning to outgrow Miliner. Their relationship soured irreparably when an argument ended with Wild reaching for a sword and hacking off one of Miliner's ears. The couple parted ways shortly afterwards. Wild paid Miliner a weekly gratuity for as long as she lived, but he was done with her. Wild gravitated toward his second mentor.

Charles Hitchin was the under-marshal of Newgate Gaol. In effect, he was one of the city's principal law enforcers, with men under his command and powers of arrest. In reality he was utterly corrupt. Having bought his rank and title for £700, he exploited it ruthlessly for financial gain. He was dandified in appearance and loved the attention of the public. From Wild's point of view, Hitchin was much better connected than Mary Miliner, having 2,000 or so criminal affiliates to exploit or work alongside. Hitchin's main source of income lay in fencing stolen goods, a profession Wild took to with enthusiasm and would reform to the point of fine art. Wild had fenced goods successfully for Miliner and had shown a greater interest and aptitude for that part of her enterprise than he ever did as her 'twang'.

The fencing profession needed a radical shake-up. Before Wild had ever set foot in London, the art of receiving stolen goods had been dealt an almost fatal blow. Between 1691 and 1706 radical changes had been made in the law and anybody caught buying or selling stolen goods could now be branded, transported for fourteen years or even hanged. Thieves still stole but there were fewer professionals to take their goods to. And those receivers that were still in the profession charged thieves exorbitant fees for their services, to mitigate the increased penalties imposed by the law. Charles Hitchin was one of the few men who still consistently operated as a receiver.

Wild had been experimenting, overhauling the receiver profession under Miliner with great success, and he now brought his ideas to Hitchin. Wild's innovation was to establish a system by which he would sell stolen objects back to the victims, having orchestrated the theft in the first place. Shortly after the theft had taken place, Wild (under the guise of a concerned civic-minded citizen) would apply to the victim stating that he knew a man that had come upon some items he believed might have been stolen and that some of the said victim's belongings might be among them. Wild would explain that he might be able to get some of these stolen items back and would ask for a list of the missing belongings. He would extract a promise from the victim that he would take no action against his friend for failing to apprehend the thieves, and he would convey that a reward for his friend would not be an imprudent thing, either.

The victim would generally go along with the proposal. The advantages would be that they would get their goods back and be spared the unpleasantness and cost of having to take the thieves to court (prosecutions being generally funded by the victim). Wild would arrange the meeting, the victim would meet Wild's middleman, money would change hands and the stolen goods would find their way back to the victim. Wild would refuse any reward offered to him personally and when the victim was gone the money would be divided proportionately between all concerned. Wild (and presumably Hitchin) would take the lion's share of the money, but the thieves still stood to make much more than they ever did under the old system (the money people were willing to pay to get their property back being sometimes half the actual value of the stolen objects). It was an adaptable system. Generally, the thefts would be at Wild's command and the stolen items would be stored in a warehouse. But if an unsolicited theft or burglary had taken place, it wasn't difficult to track the thief down and intimidate them into doing business Wild's way. Wild even had a strategy for dealing with suspicious victims who correctly suspected that Wild might be complicit in the theft. When challenged, Wild would feign offence and take the insinuation as a direct affront to his honour. He would storm off, and if the victim didn't call him back, Wild's parting shot would be to tell him where he could find him if he ever changed his mind. They generally did, and Wild's reputation amongst respectable society as the man to go to if you had been robbed began to grow.

Wild's system met with the general approbation of the criminal community. Wild was seen as intelligent, organised, tough and ruthless enough to command their respect, but generally fair to those who did business with him. He was emerging as a natural leader, whereas Hitchin was vain and markedly less intelligent than Wild. Jonathan stuck with Hitchin for two years and then set up on his own. Hitchin would have been wise to do business with Wild and accept the shift in the balance of power, but Hitchin had effectively been the cock-of-the-walk for far too long to accept what he saw as the usurpation of his position. So Hitchin went to war with Wild.

Wild vs Hitchin was a strange and polite gang war fought using pamphlets and the gutter press, the consequences of which, for the loser, would be as brutal as if guns and knives had been the weapons of choice. In 1718 Hitchin circulated a pamphlet entitled *The Regulator; or a Discovery of Thieves, Thief-Takers & co*. In it he accused Wild of applying his buckle-making skills to forgery, working as a twang, recruiting prostitutes for the purpose of training them as thieves and operating as a receiver of stolen goods. He called Wild the 'Captain-general of the army of plunderers and Ambassador Extraordinary from the Prince of the Air' – 'Prince of the Air' being one of the names given to the devil in the Bible. Most of what Hitchin had said about Wild was true, but everything that was true of Wild was mainly also true of Hitchin, with one damaging exception. Charles Hitchin was a homosexual and a prominent customer of London's gay brothels (or Molly Houses). He had even taken Wild to a Molly House when the balance of criminal power had seemed to favour Hitchin. And this was the basis of Wild's retaliation. Wild's pamphlet answered the charges levelled against him but the main focus of his attack was an exposé of Hitchin's sexual practices. Wild described his own visit to the Molly House with his benefactor, emphasising Hitchin's clear knowledge of the scene (Hitchin being referred to as 'Madam' and 'Ladyship' by many of the prostitutes). Wild assumed a tone of mock servility:

> I'll take care that no woman of the town shall walk the streets or bawdy house be kept without your Excellencies licence and trial of the ware; that no sodomitish activity shall be held without your Excellencies and making choice for your own use, in order which I'll find a female dress for your Excellency much finer than what your Excellency has been hitherto accustomed to wear …

Wild called Hitchin 'that cowardly lump of scandal'. He ended his pamphlet with a challenge to the public to test his integrity as the true, honest alternative to Hitchin, playing on the Georgian public's fear and hatred of homosexuality. What must have been an open secret had not been used as a weapon against Hitchin before, presumably because up until that point he had been too dangerous to move against. Wild was now in a position powerful enough to expose him without fear of consequences. He effectively destroyed Hitchin. Charles Hitchin was now a spent force in the underworld. His eventual end would come nine years later when he was convicted of attempted sodomy and sentenced to a £20 fine, six months in gaol and one hour in the pillory. The public were permitted to throw things at whoever was in the pillory. Generally, the projectiles were rotten vegetables, but Hitchin knew that the crowd were likely to stone him. He wore a suit of armour under his clothes but the beating he received was so severe he had to be removed from the pillory before the hour had elapsed. He died of his injuries six months later.

With Hitchin gone, London was wide open for Jonathan Wild. In truth, London had been a city under Wild's rule for quite a while before Hitchin's fatal miscalculation. Wild's reputation among legitimate society blossomed. Now he had no need to approach victims of theft or burglary. He conducted business out of an enquiry office and charged a consultation fee of 5s for anyone seeking his knowledge and advice. He organised his criminals well, partitioning London into a grid and apportioning each section to thieves whose skills and specialities were best suited to the area. To begin with, the underworld went along with Wild because his ideas were outstanding and he was a fair man to do business with, but ultimately they carried on doing business with him because they were afraid of him.

Since the beginning of his criminal career, Wild had made it his business to amass as much incriminating information as possible against anybody he came into contact with. He kept a ledger filled with his associates' names. Against many names he would put either an X or XX. A single X meant that he had enough information to see that person hanged should the need arise. XX signified that he had made up his mind to have that person hanged. But information by itself wasn't enough to secure Wild's position. He also had the manpower to enforce his will and Wild's intimate inner circle consisted of two extremely tough and violent men, Abraham Mendez and Quilt Arnold. They were his chief enforcers. Both men were fiercely loyal to their master and Wild seemed to have an uncharacteristic amount of faith in them, entrusting them with the administering of much of his empire. Wild also had a penchant for recruiting men who had absconded from the prison colonies overseas and had returned to England before their sentence had elapsed. This was a crime punishable by death and Wild used this knowledge as leverage to ensure the obedience of many of those under his command. Another recruitment technique was to catch potential criminals young. Wild inducted many of London's orphans and urchins into his street army.

Jonathan Wild used his public persona as Thief Taker General to discipline and eradicate any unruly elements within the ranks of the underworld. It wasn't enough that a Thief Taker contented himself with reuniting the burgled with their missing items, he also had to be seen to bring criminals to justice. Wild needed scalps, and any independent that refused to work with him was fair game. When an offer to do business with Wild was rejected, the thief would receive this warning: 'I have given you my word that you should come and go in safety, and so you shall; but take care of yourself for if you see me again, you see an enemy.' Wild excelled at exterminating the opposition, and when no obvious target presented itself, Wild would simply sacrifice one of his own to the gallows for appearances' sake. But Wild could also use his power to keep the loyal out of trouble if their freedom and continued service was expedient to him. So, if one of his gang were arrested and put on trial, Wild had enough professional perjurers in his employ to ensure that the felon walked free.

The year 1718 saw another challenge to Jonathan Wild's supremacy. This time the law made a belated move against him.

Not everyone in legitimate society was convinced by Wild. Admittedly, there were many who either knew or suspected that he was not all he claimed to be. In the main, these people were generally happy to let Wild exist, principally because the robbed were getting their stolen belongings back and many dangerous criminals were being tried, found guilty and executed. Ironically, on many levels, Wild was actually making the streets safe for respectable people. But there was a small contingent headed up by the solicitor-general Sir William Thompson that saw through Wild and regarded his existence and practice as an insult to the law abiding. Thompson sought to pass a law that at worst curtailed the greater part of Wild's operations, and if all went well might even see him hanged. The Act made punishable by death the practice of receiving a reward for the return of stolen property. The Act was to become known informally as The Jonathan Wild Act. Wild's response was to adapt, prosper and carry on as if the law had never been drafted.

From 1718 onwards, Wild's methods were similar to those he had used prior to the Act but with a few crucial modifications that placed a greater distance between himself, the stolen objects and any money that might change hands. The most important thing Wild did was to drop his 5s consultation fee. The victim would still meet with Wild, who would make great play of quizzing the victim for information and updating them on the progress of his investigation. Eventually, he would give the victim a price to pay his shadowy colleague for the recovery of his things, as well as a location where the transaction could take place. Sometimes, on leaving Wild's office, the victim would even be accosted by a stranger who would press a piece of paper into his hand, and written on it was the amount he ought to pay to get his goods back. If all went well the meeting would take place, the money would be paid and the goods would be returned. Wild would be thanked profusely and when the victim offered him money, he would refuse, stating that his only concern was his civic duty to the victims of crime. Whereas before 1718 Wild may have capitulated after a brief show of modesty and accepted a gratuity, he was now scrupulous in not being seen to take any kind of reward whatsoever. Behind closed doors the money was brought to Wild and he took the increasingly greater cut.

The new system worked well and Wild entered the most powerful and wealthy stage of his criminal career. He was now an incredibly rich man. He lived in a house in Little Old Bailey and would move to a larger one in Big Old Bailey. Like Hitchin before him he loved to be seen in public, sporting an expensive

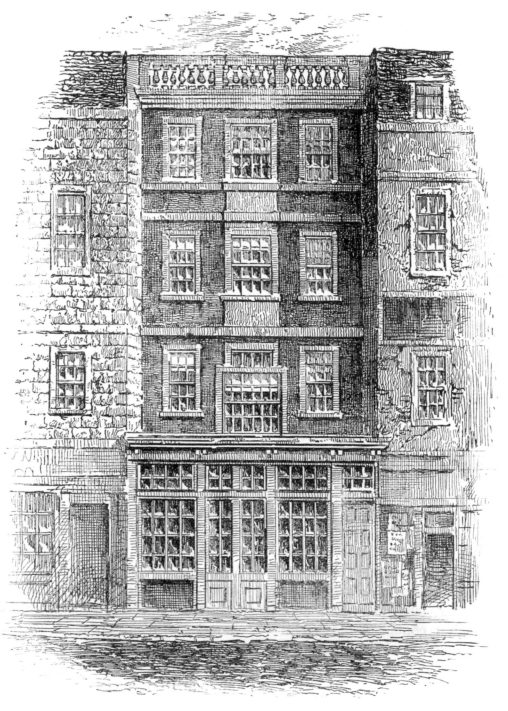

Jonathan Wild's house, bought with the proceeds of his extensive criminal activities.

wig and coat with silver buttons, carrying a sword and a silver staff with a crown on top. He worked his way through a succession of attractive women who lived with him as his wife (ignoring the fact that he had never divorced his first spouse back in Wolverhampton). He lived extravagantly and in time developed a nasty case of gout. His empire expanded: he opened up other enquiry offices, he owned warehouses full of stolen items and ran elaborate blackmail scams. He bought a sloop. He established connections in Holland and organised the sale of stolen goods overseas. In spite of The Jonathan Wild Act, the Thief Taker's standing among much of government was untarnished. Wild was even consulted by the Privy Council in 1720 about how to deal with the growing problem of highway robbery. Wild's advice was to raise the reward from £40 to £100, a move that was entirely to Wild's financial benefit as he made a point of persecuting highwaymen with an almost evangelical gusto, the highwayman being the most independent and the least servile of all Georgian criminals.

Wild's position seemed unassailable and he reigned unopposed until the mid-1720s. Wild's downfall came eventually and when it did, it wasn't the law but an ill-disciplined, treacherous rag-tag bunch of thieves that laid the foundations. The leader of the gang was a young burglar and part-time highway robber named Jack Sheppard.

SHEPPARD

Jack Sheppard was the complete inverse of Jonathan Wild. He was flamboyant, reckless, intemperate and completely lacking in most of Wild's more methodical qualities. He revelled in being a criminal and had little interest in preserving the veneer of social respectability so crucial to Wild's survival. Unlike Wild, Sheppard had a talent for getting caught, an unfortunate quality that was offset by a genius for escapology.

Sheppard was a native of London, born in White's Row, Spitalfields, in 1702. His father was a carpenter who died when Sheppard was small. Sheppard spent some time in the Bishopsgate workhouse, received a little schooling and was taken in and taught to read and write by a Mr Kneebone (a man whose kindness Sheppard would subsequently repay by robbing him). He followed his father's trade and was apprenticed to Mr Owen Wood, a Drury Lane carpenter.

Sheppard liked to drink and he liked women. To his master's consternation he spent his Sundays in the Sun Ale House in Islington. It was here that Sheppard met Joseph Hind who would introduce him to Elizabeth Lyon at the Black Lion Ale House in Drury Lane. Lyon was a thief, also known as Edgeworth Bess who, according to Sheppard, inducted him 'into a train of vices as before I was altogether a stranger to'. He hadn't known her very long before she was arrested

White's Row: Jack Sheppard's birthplace. (Mark Nightingale)

for theft and placed in the St Giles Roundhouse. Sheppard wasted no time getting her out. He found Lyon's keeper, threatened him with violence, took the keys, waltzed into the gaol and walked his mistress out.

Sheppard committed his first theft while working for Owen Wood, stealing some silver spoons from a public house in Charing Cross. His next crime of any note was also committed under his master's nose. Sheppard had been employed to either make or fit some shutters for a Mr Baines. In July 1723 he stole 24yds of cloth from Baines. Failure to sell the cloth prompted Sheppard to hide the stolen goods in a trunk at his master's house. He then had another crack at Baines' house, entering through the cellar (having loosened the wooden bars while he was working). He stole £14 worth of goods and £7 in cash. Baines' lodger was blamed for the theft but a fellow apprentice informed on Sheppard regarding the cloth he had hidden at Mr Wood's house. It was a precarious situation for a while. Sheppard was obliged to break into Wood's house and remove the cloth. Wood was keen to expose his apprentice as a thief and pressured Mr Baines to press charges. Sheppard tried to intimidate Baines into keeping his mouth shut, whilst Sheppard's mother waded in on Jack's side swearing that she had in fact bought the cloth for her son. Eventually, Sheppard was obliged to return most of the cloth but had managed to keep out of gaol.

It didn't take long before Sheppard decided he had had enough of trying to juggle the tedious demands of legitimate employment with criminal

Modern Drury Lane. Sheppard first met Edgeworth Bess in a public house on Drury Lane. (Mark Nightingale)

activity. With a year left to serve, he abandoned his apprenticeship, moved in with Edgeworth Bess and became a full-time thief. Sheppard gathered round himself a loose collection of criminal affiliates and friends who would work with him on and off. Chief among them was Joseph Blake, who was known by the strange nickname 'Blueskin' (most probably on account of his dark complexion). Blueskin Blake was a prodigious sexual athlete, a vicious man, something of a coward and by all accounts a fairly incompetent thief with a talent (that he would share with Sheppard) for getting arrested. Prior to falling in with Sheppard, Blake had run with a violent gang that had imploded in an orgy of informing and counter-informing when a series of shootings and the murder of a Chelsea pensioner had brought the full weight of the law against them. Much of the gang was hanged. Blake had co-operated with Jonathan Wild and informed on many of his associates. The Thief Taker's influence spared Blake the gallows and a sentence of transportation, but Wild couldn't keep Blake completely out of trouble and he served time in the Old Street Compter. When Blake got out he began running with Jack Sheppard.

Sheppard was arrested for the first time at a pub in Seven Dials. He had recently robbed another pub with his brother Tom. Jack and Tom had neglected to obtain permission from Jonathan Wild to carry out the robbery and consequently hadn't paid their tithe to him. Tom was arrested. He informed on his brother to the Thief Taker. Sheppard was waiting in the pub for a man who was going to play skittles with him for money; he had been told by an associate that the man was an easy mark and ripe for a fleecing. The man turned out to be the constable of St Giles' Parish. The person who had brokered the meeting was James 'Hell and Fury' Sykes, an agile and tough enforcer of Wild's. Sheppard was locked up on the second floor of St Giles Roundhouse for the night. A justice would question him in the morning. As far as Wild was concerned, another upstart had been made an example of and the status quo had been re-established.

It took Sheppard three hours to escape from St Giles.

Sheppard had been admitted to the Roundhouse at around six in the evening. He had on his person an old razor, which he used to cut a hole in the roof. He placed his bed under the hole in order to catch any of the noisy debris that fell to the ground. By nine o'clock he had made a hole just about big enough to squeeze through. In an effort to force himself on to the roof, he dislodged a tile or a brick. The loose object slid over the edge of the roof and fell into the street, hitting a passer-by on the head. Sheppard had inadvertently attracted an audience. He forced himself on to the rooftop and dropped down into the churchyard. He scaled another wall and lost himself in the crowd. It was a reasonably spectacular breakout, but better was to follow.

Sheppard enjoyed a short spell of freedom before being arrested again. This time he was caught pickpocketing. He was locked in New Prison,

The site of New Prison, Clerkenwell. (Mark Nightingale)

Jack Sheppard escapes from New Prison, Clerkenwell, with Edgeworth Bess on his back. (Illustrated by Stephen Dennis)

Clerkenwell, being put in the condemned hold and chained up. Edgeworth Bess had also been arrested. Sheppard and Bess were put in the same cell as the authorities were under the misapprehension that the couple were man and wife. Both prisoners were allowed visitors and someone (in all probability Blake) managed to smuggle a tool in. This was all Sheppard needed to remove his fetters. Sheppard then began to work one of the bars on the cell window loose, and he and Bess climbed the 20ft or so down into the yard using an improvised rope made from prison bedding.

The next obstacle in their way was a 25ft wall. Bess clambered onto Sheppard's back and the thief climbed the wall without the aid of a rope or ladder, the locks and bolts acting as hand and foot holds. The two of them thereby climbed over the wall and made it safely to the street below and liberty. They parted company. Sheppard enjoyed a three-month hiatus from capture before he was taken for a third time.

Sheppard and Blake decided to rob Sheppard's old benefactor, Mr Kneebone. They stole £50 worth of cloth but had trouble trying to fence their haul. Their choice of fence was William Field, a pathologically treacherous man who, unbeknown to them, was one of Wild's informers. Field stole their cloth, went to Wild and began to tell tales.

Jack Sheppard was not a difficult man to catch. The notion of a low profile was a concept more than slightly alien to him. He was addicted to the same locales and drinking spots, and was cavalier in his defiance of Wild. He was also an appalling judge of criminal character with a deeply unreliable circle of friends. In July 1724 he was taken for the second time by Jonathan Wild. The Thief Taker met up with Edgeworth Bess and got her drunk. She gave away her lover's whereabouts without too much persuasion and Wild sent Quilt Arnold to bring Sheppard in. Sheppard was incarcerated for the first time in Newgate Gaol.

Newgate had been a hated fixture of London topography since the Middle Ages. The gaol had assumed many different forms in its lifetime. It had crumbled and had been rebuilt. It had burned down in the Great Fire and had been rebuilt again. It had survived all of nature's assaults to stand symbolic of the worst that the establishment could mete out on those that chose to flaunt its laws. It was a desperately overcrowded place that incubated disease. It was fortress-like, labyrinthine in design and believed to be impossible to escape from.

Sheppard was put on trial at the Old Bailey. Both Wild and Kneebone stood witness against him. Sheppard was found guilty, sentenced to death and placed in the condemned cell. Surprisingly, Sheppard was allowed visitors. This wasn't deemed to be too much of a problem as the cell door was thick and sturdy. There was an opening at the top of the door but it was lined with metal spikes. Visitors were allowed as far as the door but not inside the cell. As Sheppard's friends came to wish him farewell, one of them managed to smuggle a tool to Sheppard past the spikes. Sheppard began to work one of the spikes loose.

On 30 August the warrant for Sheppard's death was issued. On the same day he was visited by two women. The guards were either drinking or else were distracted by one of the two visitors, and Sheppard managed to remove a spike, climb through the opening and literally walk out of Newgate. He and his two accomplices caught a Hackney Cab and disappeared into London.

Sheppard lasted ten or so days before being rearrested on Finchley Common. He had even left London at the behest of his friends and stayed in Northampton for a short while, but came back when the family he was staying with failed to treat him with the adulation he felt he deserved. Sheppard was taken back to Newgate and placed in the 'Castle', the most secure part of the prison. This time there were no visitors and Sheppard was handcuffed and chained to the ground.

A condemned cell in Newgate Gaol. Both Sheppard and Wild were held in cells like these before their respective executions at Tyburn.

Jonathan Wild must have felt that the tiresome and distracting war with this resourceful company of independents was finally coming to an end. Joseph 'Blueskin' Blake had also been captured. Wild, along with Abraham Mendez and Quilt Arnold, had personally arrested him. Blake had shown a degree of defiance in capture, threatening to kill Quilt Arnold with a penknife, but submitted to Quilt when he threatened to cut Blake's arm off. Blake was locked up in Newgate and put on trial. Wild, Field, Mendez and Arnold all gave testimony against him and he was found guilty and sentenced to death. At Blake's request, Wild came to see him at Newgate, and the two men met in the yard. Blake pleaded with Wild to use his influence to get his sentence commuted from death to transportation. Wild refused. Blake had a small penknife hidden on his person. He grabbed Wild's neck and cut his throat. The point of the blade entered the skin just below Wild's ear and Blake dragged the knife across the windpipe. Wild was wearing a muslin stock around his neck so the blade was hampered and missed cutting any arteries or the windpipe. Blake was quickly restrained and Jonathan Wild, soaked in his own blood, was rushed to the surgeons. Newgate was in shock. Prisoners were dizzy at the prospect that Jonathan Wild might actually be dead and Newgate's gaolers had their hands full restoring order. As a consequence, Sheppard was not properly watched.

No one really knows how he did it, but Sheppard removed his handcuffs and somehow managed to break the chain between his legs and loose himself from the anchor that secured him to the floor. The irons around his ankles were pulled up and tied off to stop them impeding his movement. There was a chimney in his cell that offered a possible route out of the prison. Sheppard fitted himself inside the chimney and began to climb upwards. An iron bar blocked his way. He used bits of the chain he had broken to dig the iron bar out of the chimney wall. He carried on climbing a little further upwards and then used the bar to smash a hole through the chimney wall into an adjacent room. The room was called The Red Room. It was situated directly above the Castle and was completely empty.

Sheppard had broken into a deserted part of Newgate that hadn't been in use for over half a decade. The Red Room was locked from the outside. Sheppard broke the lock, only to find a succession of locked doors and empty rooms between him and freedom. He alternated between brute force and delicate craftsmanship as he employed the iron bar and a nail he had found to spring locks or smash holes through walls to get at bolts. He passed through a chapel and broke off an iron spike adding it to his impromptu tool kit. The noise Sheppard was making was cacophonous, but the cells and corridors Sheppard passed through were empty and the din didn't seem to attract any unwanted attention. Mercifully, the last door was bolted from the inside. Sheppard drew the bolt and stepped into the fresh air. He could see London below him.

Joseph 'Blueskin' Blake cuts Jonathan Wild's throat at Newgate Gaol. (Illustrated by Stephen Dennis)

The time that had elapsed from the moment Jack Sheppard slipped his cuffs until he stood on Newgate's outer wall was five hours. Sheppard considered how to get down to the street. He needed a rope and he hadn't thought to fashion one and bring it with him. He retraced his steps, climbed back down into his cell and grabbed his blankets. He climbed up the chimney again and weaved his way back to the final open door. He stuck the metal spike into the prison wall, tied his blanket rope to the spike and climbed down the side of Newgate, settling on the rooftop of a neighbouring house. Sheppard entered the house and rested for two hours. The house was occupied and Sheppard nearly gave himself away as he snuck down the stairs and let himself out onto the street. He weaved his way through London, passing through Holborn and Grey's Inn Lane, arriving at Tottenham Court around two o'clock in the morning. He found what looked like a deserted house in a nearby field and slept for three hours.

When Sheppard woke up it was raining. It was a Friday morning and he was hungry. The fetters had made a mess of his legs and needed to be removed. He stayed where he was until nightfall then put on a long coat that hid the chains from view and left the house, going into Tottenham. He had 40s on him and

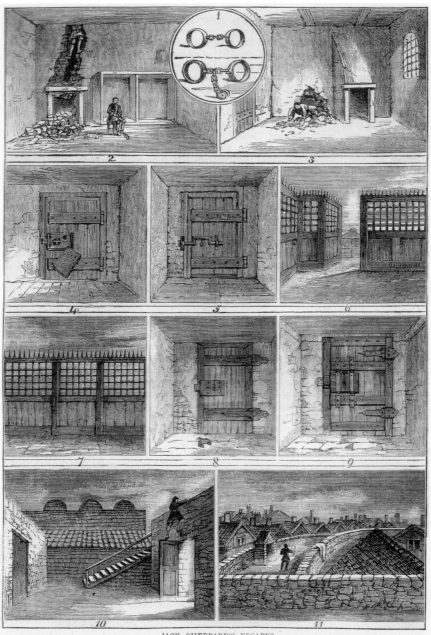

JACK SHEPPARD'S ESCAPES.

1. Handcuffs and Feetlocks, and Padlock to Ground. 2. Cell over the Castle, Jack Sheppard fastened to the floor. Climbing up the Chimney, where he found a bar of iron. 3. Red Room over the Castle, into which he got out of the Chimney. 4. Door of the Red Room, the lock of which he put back. 5. Door of the Entry between the Red Room and the Chapel. 6. Door going into the Chapel, which he burst open. 7. Door going out of the Chapel towards the Leads. 8. Door with a Spring Lock, which he opened. 9. Door over the same Passage. 10. The Lower Leads. 11. The Higher Leads, the walls of which he got over, and descended by the staircase off the roof of a turner's house into the street.

Jack Sheppard's second escape from Newgate Gaol.

Jack Sheppard begins his second escape from Newgate by climbing up the inside of a chimney and digging his way into an unoccupied cell with an iron bar. (Illustrated by Stephen Dennis)

managed to buy some food. With the exception of a return trip to Tottenham for more food, Sheppard spent Saturday recuperating. He found a stone and tried unsuccessfully to smash the irons loose.

He was surprised by the arrival of the owner of the house and had to think quickly to avoid a violent incident and recapture. He lied but had the sense to pepper his lie with a little of the truth. He confessed that he was a fugitive but that the reason for his imprisonment was because he had fathered an illegitimate child. Sheppard was lucky. The owner of the property not only believed him, but had once been in a similar position himself and was sympathetic. The owner wouldn't give Jack away but he wanted him off his property as soon as possible. Sheppard moved on.

The sob story had worked once and Sheppard used it again on a cobbler. The cobbler believed Sheppard and agreed to help him remove his irons. The fetters were Sheppard's final impediment. With the leg irons gone he could

Sheppard, after escaping from Newgate, persuades a shoemaker to knock his irons off. (*The Newgate Calendar*, Vol. 1, J. Robins & Co., 1824)

pass his dishevelled appearance off as that of a beggar and begin to enjoy his freedom. News of what he had done began to break all over London and he went on an incognito tour eavesdropping on the public as they chewed over his great exploit. He listened to balladeers who were already setting his adventure to verse. He even discussed the escape with a woman in a Rupert Street pub who had no idea who she was talking to.

Sheppard kept a reasonably low profile for a short while. His mother entreated him to leave London for his own safety. Sheppard told her that he would do as she wished, but as soon as he caught the scent of his old haunts and all the fun and excitement that they promised, he went back to work.

SHEPPARD VS WILD

Sheppard's second escape from Newgate ensured his criminal canonisation. It had also marked him out as Jonathan Wild's arch-enemy and principal target for destruction. Sheppard's Newgate escapes were tantamount to repeatedly spitting in Wild's face. Although prompted mainly by a pressing desire not to be hanged, Sheppard must have been fully aware that he was holding the Thief Taker General up to ridicule every time he broke out of prison. For his part, Wild would always be able to catch Jack Sheppard, and it would only be a matter of time before Sheppard presented the Thief Taker with another opportunity to secure and hang him. But what Wild failed to understand was that with every attempt to secure and hang Sheppard, and every corresponding escape attempt that followed, Wild was making a vital contribution to Sheppard's ever-growing status as a living 'folk-hero'. He was also increasingly casting himself as the villain in the eyes of the public, whose support was essential to his survival. Wild's obsessive pursuit of Sheppard began to look to all and sundry more and more like the personal vendetta it actually was. The normally astute Thief Taker was becoming increasingly blind to the overall context of his actions. Moreover Wild failed to see that at this point hanging Sheppard would be tantamount to martyring him.

Sheppard was captured for the final time in October 1724. He had spent the night drinking, going from alehouse to alehouse seeing many of his friends who were astounded at his lack of discretion and advised him to be more circumspect. Sheppard was arrested at midnight, too drunk to do anything other than comply with his captors. He was taken back to Newgate and placed in a secure cell where he was weighed down with chains and watched like a hawk.

His celebrity had skyrocketed since his last escape. There was a clamour among respectable society to see with their own eyes the exotic thief before he either escaped again or was hanged. Ironically, considering the risks to the prison's reputation should Sheppard break out for a third time, Newgate permitted him the luxury of visitors. There was an ulterior motive. For Sheppard's gaolers the financial rewards outweighed the risks and they charged an admission fee for every visitor who wanted to see the famous thief. Amongst the many affluent and well-to-do people who took an interest in Jack Sheppard, the writer Daniel Defoe and the pugilist James Figgs both visited him at Newgate. Nevertheless, the security measures taken were thorough. No visitor was allowed any physical contact with Sheppard and great pains were taken to ensure that nothing could be smuggled to him. This time Sheppard was secured with 300lb of metal.

Jack Sheppard and Joseph Blake were both in Newgate and due to be executed. Blake had been unrepentant concerning his actions. He boasted that his only regret was that his knife had not been large and sharp enough to behead the Thief Taker General. Blueskin's bravado deserted him in the days leading up to his hanging. He cried at chapel, drank a lot and wept almost up to the point of execution. In early November he was hanged. A few days later Jack Sheppard made his own journey from Newgate to Tyburn gallows. Twenty thousand people were present and the immense crowd were publically conspicuous in their support of Jack Sheppard as he was strangled to death.

What should have been Wild's great victory had been horribly inverted. He had been maimed by his prisoner and was lucky not to have been murdered. A popular ballad had even been written celebrating Blake's act of violence. Sheppard and Blake were in the ground, but Wild had been exposed to his enemies as fallible and vulnerable to attack. Worse than that, the public held him in contempt, judging him personally responsible for Sheppard's death. Wild recovered from his injuries but in time would be quoted as lamenting the fact that Blake had not killed him when he'd had the chance. On many levels business went on as usual. But Wild had changed. There was an increasingly haywire quality to his normally impeccable judgement and he began to personally involve himself in matters best left to his subordinates.

A problem arose concerning one of Wild's European enterprises. Not everybody whose belongings Wild arranged to have stolen approached him to have them returned. Consequently, Wild often found himself with a surfeit of stolen goods that needed to be offloaded. For this purpose he would have his sloop sail to the Netherlands and sell the goods there. The man in charge of the sloop was Roger Johnson. Johnson had accused one of the crew of stealing from Wild. The sailor took the accusation personally and sought revenge. Johnson also had another enemy in the form of a thief named Thomas Edwards. The offended sailor and Thomas Edwards colluded to bring Johnson down. They informed on both Wild and Johnson, and their information led to one of Wild's warehouses being searched.

Wild stayed out of prison but his goods were confiscated. He couldn't let the challenge go unanswered. He arrested Edwards, but the prisoner was bailed out and retaliated by having Johnson arrested. Johnson was temporarily detained by constables at a pub in Whitechapel when word got back to Wild. Wild arrived in person at the pub with Quilt Arnold. The two men started a brawl. In the confusion of the bar fight Johnson slipped away. Wild left Whitechapel and went to ground for three weeks. When the Thief Taker surfaced, he figured that the dust had settled sufficiently for him to go about his business, but he was wrong. On 15 February 1725, Jonathan Wild was arrested by the High Constable of Holborn and charged with helping Roger Johnson escape from custody. Wild was sent to Newgate. While he was in custody, a 'warrant of detainer' was produced against him listing eleven separate charges. The warrant read like an A–Z of everything bad Jonathan Wild had ever done.

Amazingly, considering the unprecedented nature of the move against him and the precarious position he had found himself in, Wild carried on conducting his business from prison. He negotiated the return of £50 worth of

The disgraced Jonathan Wild is taken to Tyburn in a cart.

Marble Arch stands where Tyburn used to be. Tyburn was one of London's principal locations for public execution. Both Jack Sheppard and Jonathan Wild were hanged at here. (*Three Hundred and Sixty-Five Views of London*, Rock Bros Ltd)

lace that had been stolen (at Wild's command) from a Katherine Steatham. Wild foolishly allowed himself to be in the same place as the victim when she was in possession of the 10-guinea reward he had manipulated out of her. The hedge of middlemen that had always insulated Wild from his signature crime was absent. So when the two thieves Wild had ordered to steal the lace turned on him, and Katherine Steatham testified as to the transaction that had taken place in Newgate, there was little Wild could do to refute the charge. The Thief Taker was indicted under The Jonathan Wild Act for receiving money for the recovery of stolen goods. Wild had destroyed himself.

To be fair to Wild, his time was almost over anyway; he merely hastened his own departure. The stolen lace aside, there was still the original indictments to be dealt with. His public support had gone. The government had finally woken up to the true nature of the person that they had entrusted with policing the capital and were eager to be rid of him. Thieves were lining up to testify against him, motivated by personal revenge, a desire to save their own skins if they were already in custody, or because they had simply wearied of Wild's tyrannical monopoly. During his trial Wild hardly bothered to refute any of the charges. His defence rested on a plea for clemency based on the number of criminals he had brought to justice. It was a perversely spirited but futile effort. Wild was found guilty and sentenced to hang.

Wild wrote to the king asking for a pardon. He received no reply. He laboured under the delusion that rescue would come by way of the establishment. He was politely ignored. His behaviour at Newgate was erratic: he refused to go to chapel for fear of being insulted by the other convicts; he refused to eat; and he became obsessed with the state of the soul immediately after the moment of death, but showed no interest in repentance. On the night before the hanging he overdosed on laudanum. The intervention of prisoners, combined with an empty stomach, induced a vomiting fit, denying Wild the more peaceful death.

In the morning Wild, groggy and feeble, was put on the cart and led to Tyburn gallows. The crowd despised him. From Newgate to Tyburn Wild was pelted with mud and stones; they taunted him and swore at him. By the time Wild reached Tyburn his head had cleared. The hangman was kind under the circumstances; he offered Wild some time to gather his thoughts and prepare himself for death. The crowd took offence and threatened the hangman with violence if he didn't make haste and kill the Thief Taker quickly. The hangman's nerve failed him and Jonathan Wild was rushed onto the gallows and hanged in front of a jubilant and rabid audience.

Wild and Sheppard were both dead, but the great feud had only just begun.

2

THE GREAT FEUD:
IN PRINT

'Everything comes in circles, even Professor Moriarty. Jonathan Wild was the hidden force of the London criminals, to whom he sold his brains and his organisation on a fifteen percent commission. The old wheel turns and the same spokes come up. It's all been done before and will be again.'

The Valley of Fear, Arthur Conan Doyle

DANIEL DEFOE & THE GRUB STREET PRESS

Sheppard and Wild's first lasting literary incarnation came courtesy of the novelist Daniel Defoe. Defoe was reaching the end of his remarkable life and career. He had just finished his run of innovative and form-defining novels, comprising amongst others *Robinson Crusoe* and *Moll Flanders*. Defoe was making his living as a writer for John Applebee's publishing house. Applebee was the mogul of what had come to be known as the Grub Street Press. Grub Street was a notorious avenue in London famous for crime. It was also the less-than-flattering moniker given to the thriving pamphlet industry. Grub Street tapped into a deep hunger among the emerging middle class for cheap, disposable, true crime literature. Grub Street produced biographical pamphlets and chronicled in newspapers the misdeeds of all the most fashionable criminals. By and large the pamphlets were sensationalised works exaggerating the exploits of criminals, turning Georgian sociopaths into flamboyant folk heroes. Naturally, the underworld approved and there was both blatant and tacit collusion between criminals and the press, to the point of thieves occasionally tailoring their crimes to attract the attention of Grub Street.

Daniel Defoe.

Sometimes business arrangements were struck between Grub Street and their criminal subjects. A thief in Newgate might offer his or her story to Grub Street. The story would regularly be dictated to a Grub Street journalist who would act as a ghostwriter. But more often than not a criminal's last confession was completely invented by a writer who wasn't present and hadn't met their subject. Many pamphleteers made claims to the authenticity of their work, citing access to secret papers of the condemned. It was mostly nonsense. The Grub Street Press was therefore looked down on by many of the more sophisticated members of the burgeoning London literati. Defoe was the exception. His output and movement between literary genres had been consistantly varied. He had always been a fertile pamphleteer, and crime and the causes of crime had been a subject of great interest to him throughout his career; his novel *Moll Flanders* being considered one of the most credible fictional depictions of the English underworld up to that time. Defoe's own experience also lent weight and credibility to his pamphlet writing as he had once been a prisoner at Newgate. But what really set Defoe apart from his Grub Street peers (with the obvious exception of his literary genius) was the absence of sensationalism in his work, as well as its relative historical accuracy. Defoe was a moralist who scorned the satirical and exaggerated leanings of the average Grub Street hack. He considered his works moral tracts rather than pamphlets, and it is commonly believed that Defoe wrote two works concerning Jonathan Wild and Jack Sheppard.

SHEPPARD & DEFOE

The first of these works, *A History of the Remarkable Life of Sheppard*, was written while Sheppard was alive and at large, commemorating his second escape from Newgate Gaol. Naturally, Sheppard loved Grub Street. He revelled in his own mythology, and theories and legends persist as to the closeness of his relationship with Applebee and Defoe. He was said to have personally delivered a letter to Applebee incognito, teasing the publisher that now that he was free, Applebee would not be able to further capitalise on his fame by printing the thief's final speech before hanging. When Sheppard was in Newgate for the final time, Applebee did, in fact, publish his last confession.

A Narrative of all Robberies, Escapes &c. of John Sheppard was a first-person account almost certainly ghosted by Defoe. The writer's hand is most evident in the self-reflective and semi-repentant spin he puts on Sheppard's account of his own villainies: 'And it will be no small satisfaction to me to think that I have thoroughly purg'd my conscience before I leave the world, and make reparation to many persons injured by me, as far as is in my power'; sentiments the preening and narcissistic thief showed very little evidence of in the run-up to his execution.

A grisly postscript to the relationship between Applebee and Sheppard exists that may have inadvertently contributed to Sheppard's death (and would certainly explain the ease with which he held court in the weeks preceding his hanging). A deal was apparently struck between Applebee and Sheppard regarding his death. When anybody was executed, their body was required to dangle on the scaffold for fifteen minutes before any attempt was made to cut them down. In the days before the long drop broke a felon's neck, death would occur as a result of strangulation. It was a slow and painful way to die. But from time to time there were those that survived the fifteen minutes and were cut down by friends, whisked away somewhere private and revived. Sheppard believed he could resist the noose and stay alive for those fifteen minutes. He is thought to have promised Applebee that if the publisher could arrange to cut him down and revive him, then he would give him an exclusive interview. Applebee agreed and made the necessary preparations (even enlisting Defoe to help him). If this story is true then Sheppard was the butt of a divine black joke. The hangmen suspended the thief in mid-air and his fifteen minutes of agony began. Applebee and Defoe had arranged for a hearse to take the body away the moment the quarter-hour had elapsed. But Jack Sheppard's public deliberately blocked the progress of the hearse thinking its intention was to take their hero's body away to be dissected for the purposes of medical instruction (a common fate amongst the condemned). In the mind of the mob this was an unacceptable violation. It was an entirely unhelpful act of compassion, and if the story is true then Sheppard's public ensured his demise. He might even have appreciated the irony.

DEFOE & WILD

When any great criminal fell there was a feeding frenzy among the hacks to be the first to produce an account of their execution, and Defoe was thought to have written one of the many versions of Jonathan Wild's hanging to be published almost immediately after the event. He had a second crack at Wild two weeks later when *The True Life and Genuine Account of the Life of Jonathan Wild* was published. Two weeks after the hanging was normally considered too late to be of commercial relevance to a self-respecting Grub Street publisher. But Defoe's agenda was different. He began by distancing himself from his contemporaries, referring to 'several absurd and ridiculous tracts' and their 'jesting tone'. He expressed contempt for the way in which Wild's life had been made 'a kind of romance before his face'. Whereas his tract contained a detailed analysis of Wild's working methods. Defoe even placed himself within the narrative, recounting a consultation he had had with Wild when trying to recover a modestly valuable silver-hilted sword that had been stolen from him (an item Wild failed to recover, presumably due to its lack of market value). Defoe expressed his disgust at every turn with the hypocrisy and ruthlessness of Wild's criminal strategies, from recruiting children to his habit of hanging his contemporaries for the purpose of maintaining a veneer of propriety, a practice Defoe interpreted as a form of mass murder.

Defoe's tract contained few of the juicy anecdotes that punctuated the Thief Taker's life. He was more interested in exploring the new criminal animal that society had produced in the person of Jonathan Wild. In the intricate layers of organisation and subterfuge with which Wild built and maintained his empire, Defoe recognised in the Thief Taker an extraordinary criminal anomaly, with no precedent before it and, in Defoe's opinion, one unlikely to be repeated again. 'The life of Jonathan Wild is a perfectly new scene,' he said.

SHEPPARD & WILD, WALPOLE & GAY

In 1728 Wild and Sheppard would assume surrogate identities and their feud would be set to music. *The Beggar's Opera* grew out of a conversation between the poet John Gay and the novelist Jonathan Swift. Both men were members of the Scriblerus Club, a loose collective of artists unified by a desire to satirise their peers and the Whig government. The majority of the Club's members were Tory and united by a deep antipathy towards the First Lord of the Treasury, Sir Robert Walpole. Swift suggested to Gay the possibility of writing a 'Newgate Pastoral'. Pastorals were a popular theatrical genre in which one form of society acted as a metaphor for another for the purposes of ridicule. Town and Country Pastorals were the predominant examples of this type of theatre. The notion of creating a pastoral populated by figures from the London underworld was a radical and inviting challenge to John Gay. The possibilities for satire and score settling were legion.

The theatrical scene in Georgian London was embarrassing for a city that had nurtured Shakespeare, his contemporaries and the waves of talented playwrights that had flourished in the Jacobean and Restoration eras. The anarchic and violent poetry of the Jacobean age, as well as the poetic sexual licence of Restoration comedy, had now been replaced by a moribund creative conservatism. Italian opera dominated the London stage and lengthy arias sung by noble, often mythical heroes and heroines were the staples of Georgian theatrical entertainment. *The Beggar's Opera* would subvert all of this.

Gay drew heavily on the example of Jonathan Wild for his main character Peachum, a powerful Thief Taker and receiver of stolen goods. Peachum and his wife run their criminal empire in much the same manner that Wild had ruled London. In the first act Peachum thumbs through a ledger deliberating which of his subordinates should be hanged and which should be spared, just as Wild might have done when he was alive. Jack Sheppard found his own alternative in the highwayman Captain Macheath (the nearest *The Beggar's Opera* comes to having a romantic lead). The dispute between Peachum and Macheath provides the main conflict, which is at the centre of *The Beggar's Opera*. But unlike the real feud, the cause of the tension between the two criminals is not jurisdiction but a woman. Peachum's daughter Polly has fallen in love with Macheath and she intends to marry him. Her parents violently object to their only daughter's marriage on the basis that it has no monetary advantage, and they seek to have Macheath hanged. Macheath has no intention of actually marrying Polly however, and is involved with at least two other women (including Lucy Locket, the daughter of Newgate's chief gaoler) and is happy to juggle their affections. Peachum has Macheath committed to Newgate and when Macheath escapes, Peachum recaptures him. Macheath is sent to the gallows to the consternation of his rivals in love, the mob that adores him and a small gathering of women, some of whom present him with his bastard offspring.

Apart from the obvious entertainment value of a London public watching on a London stage recognisable outlaw figures from extremely recent history, the possibility of an insulting metaphor was irresistible for a man with a multitude of axes to grind, and John Gay was a creatively vindictive artist with many enemies. For starters, Gay was keen to hold the conventions of Italian

The 'Great Man', Sir Robert Walpole.

opera up for ridicule and subversion. Instead of the standard elongated arias and duets, each musical number was deliberately condensed. The melodies were not original but a recognisable mixture of popular ballads and snatches of opera (mainly Handel, the one universally respected artistic figure of the time). Gay set his own words to *Greensleeves* and *Over the Hills and Far Away*.

The musical highpoint of Gay's dynamic second act was a thieves' chorus, 'Fill your Glasses, Let us Take the Road', performed to the tune of a march from Handel's opera *Rinaldo*.

It wasn't just the form of Italian opera that Gay was subverting, but the grotesque deference shown to its stars. Polly Peachum and Lucy Locket's spiteful duet lampooned the public hatred between Francesca Curzoni and Faustina Bordoni, two warring sopranos. Peachum and Locket also stood for the antagonistic mistresses of George I. As the king was dead and his recently crowned son held little love or respect for his father, this was perhaps not as cavalier a move as it first appeared. But Gay reserved his fiercest scorn for the First Lord of the Treasury, Sir Robert Walpole, a man for whom the consequences of offence carried great risk for the poet.

To anybody watching the first performances of *The Beggar's Opera*, the dual appeal would have been seeing the dramatised exploits of Jonathan Wild (a man whose hanging much of the audience may well have attended) and recognising their own chief minister blatantly caricatured as a treacherous thief and slippery dispenser of bribes.

Robert Walpole was a Norfolk man from a rich family. He was educated at Eton and King's College, Cambridge. He became an MP in 1701, a Whig in a predominantly Tory environment. He had his enemies and did well to survive, being impeached for corruption and put in the Tower of London for treason. When Queen Anne died without leaving an heir, her Hanoverian successor George I whittled away the Tory majority to virtually nothing, paving the way for a Whig monopoly. But the Whig party was too riddled with factions to properly establish political dominance. The infighting was so pervasive that Walpole and his main political ally and brother-in-law, Charles Townsend, joined the Tories for a season in order to harass enemies within their own party. In 1720 Walpole returned to the fold and eventually emerged as an ambivalent saviour figure during one of the worst financial crises in English history.

The South Sea Company had been established in 1711. It was a Tory venture designed to provide a commercial alternative to the Bank of England and the East India Company, both Whig enterprises. England's national debt had been dangerously inflated by its involvement in the mammoth and expensive War of Spanish Succession that had raged across Europe in the opening years of the new century. A strategy began to develop by which government investment in the South Sea Company could be used as a way of reducing the national debt, which stood at £50 million. Of their projected profits, the South Sea Company reckoned the debt could be reduced by £9 million, but for the scheme to work a law had to be passed that permitted national debt stock to be swapped for South Sea Company stock. For this to happen, numerous powerful and influential people had to be convinced that the scheme was viable and in their financial interests. The easiest way to achieve this was bribery. South Sea Company stock was sold cheaply or simply given to power brokers to ensure their support. The knock-on effect was speculation frenzy. The rush to buy Company stock, combined with a demand for quick profits, very swiftly made the situation financially unsustainable. The value of stock rose at a mouth-watering rate, but when the more powerful investors began to cash in, the stock started to plunge in value. The consequence came to be known as the Bursting of the South Sea Bubble. Entire fortunes were obliterated, with many investors losing everything they had. Some ruined participants in the scheme killed themselves and others left the country in disgrace.

Walpole had never approved of the scheme. He had been in favour of using the more financially stable Bank of England to assume much of the debt, but he had been ignored. With the economy in tatters, however, Parliament now turned to him for a solution. Walpole sought to shield the national debt by doing a variation on what he had initially suggested. He persuaded the Bank of England and the East India Company to take on £9 million worth

The Bank of England. (*Mysteries of Police & Crime*, Vol. III, Cassell and Company Ltd)

of South Sea stock, stabilising its value. He also compensated national debt stockholders as much as he was able. It was a phenomenal piece of manoeuvring that saved the country from further damage. But relative stability had its price. Walpole's measures allowed many officials to walk away from the mess that they had personally engineered, thereby avoiding possible criminal charges. Walpole was perceived by his enemies to have deliberately shielded many of the worst offenders in order to save the face of his government. From that point on his reputation for corruption (whether deserved or not) was permanently established in the eyes of many. Not that Walpole was overly concerned. He was the man of the hour. The Whig party was as unified as it had ever recently been and Walpole was now its de facto leader with the backing of the king. An added bonus was the fact that Walpole's main enemies in the party had been some of the chief architects of the South Sea crisis and amongst the few whose careers had been conveniently ruined by it. Those that hated Walpole created a term of abuse designed to mock his position. The facetious title bestowed upon him was 'Prime Minister'.

John Gay had personal reasons for despising Walpole. Gay had had ambitions to advance at Court. He had what should have been powerful friends in royal circles, but all of them were out of favour with Walpole and Walpole's

The Lincoln's Inn Fields Theatre was the location of a spectacular brawl between actors and the audience. (Illustrated by Stephen Dennis)

power base was so secure that unless he liked you, or saw profit in his association with you, you would not be advanced. The best position Gay could glean
from his contacts was the poultry office of gentleman usher to Princess Luisa.
The Beggar's Opera was written shortly after this rebuff, most probably in a
spirit of personal recrimination.

The Beggar's Opera was to be staged at The Lincoln's Inn Fields Theatre.
It was presided over by the actor manager John Rich, one of the great theatrical pioneers of the age and Gay's business partner. The theatre had hosted
some radical innovations in the staging of entertainments. The pantomime,
moving scenery and the first use of the proscenium arch had all been introduced to the English stage by way of Lincoln's Inn Fields. On a poetic level
it was the perfect arena for the rough new work that was about to captivate
London, as seven years previously Lincoln's Inn Fields had been the scene of
a spectacular brawl between actors and drunken aristocrats in the audience.

Walpole personally attended the first night of *The Beggar's Opera*. He had an
ambivalent relationship with the arts to say the least. He had been a successful
art collector and had sold all he had to Catherine II of Russia. He appeared to
have bad taste in poetry but hated writers, which was natural considering his
fiercest critics were many of the best writers of the age. He did like music and
for that reason may have approached *The Beggar's Opera* with his guard more
lowered than normal.

The Beggar's Opera is introduced in the form of a conversation between the
characters Beggar and Player, who explain the new form of entertainment the
audience are about to witness. As the play begins in earnest, John Gay sets out
his stall with his first song. As Peachum sits pouring over his ledger, the first
verses the audience hear the Wild/Walpole doppelganger sing are:

> Through all the employments of life, Each neighbour abuses his brother;
> Whore and rogue, they call husband and wife: All professions be rogue to
> one another. The priest calls the lawyer a cheat: The lawyer be-knaves the
> divine: And the statesman, because he's so great, Thinks his trade is as honest
> as mine.

The first spoken words the audience hears Peachum speak are:

> A lawyer is an honest employment, so is mine. Like me too, he acts in a
> double capacity, both against rogues, and for 'em; for it is but fitting that we
> should protect and encourage cheats since we live by them.

Both songs and libretto set the tone for the rubbishing Walpole and his friends
would receive over the course of the next two or so hours.

The public loved it. They loved the satire, the deflating of operatic self-indulgence, the recognition of popular songs, the murky characters and street language, and the chance to hate Wild and hero-worship Sheppard all over again. They were even treated to a happy ending as Macheath's hanging is interrupted by an epilogue between Player and Beggar, where the two agree to change the inevitable grimness of the ending in favour of something more traditional, happy, fairytale-esque and operatic. Gay had his cake and ate it. It was a last satiric dig at the bloated and dramatically lazy conventions of opera, as well as the rewriting of history regarding Jack Sheppard that the public wanted.

The success of *The Beggar's Opera* was enormous and Rich and Gay made a fortune. Considering most plays of the time's natural first-run lifespan was a handful of performances, *The Beggar's Opera* ran for sixty-two nights and has been in and out of the theatrical repertoire ever since. Almost a hundred years later, the great critic and essayist William Hazlitt said this of *The Beggar's Opera*:

> It is a vulgar error to call this a vulgar play ... The elegance of the composition is in exact proportion to the coarseness of the materials: by 'happy alchemy of mind', the author has extracted an essence of refinement from the dregs of human life and turned its very dross into gold.

As for Walpole, he took his beating in public with sufficient rectitude and bided his time.

Wild and Sheppard would be resurrected again but they would go their separate ways for a season. They would resume their feud properly in the next century, but for the time being their isolated examples would serve a duo of painters and a writer, and Walpole would be offended again and again and again.

FIELDING & WILD

No single writer did more to provoke Walpole than Henry Fielding, who took up the baton of John Gay and the Scriblerus Club to repeatedly rubbish Walpole in a series of theatrical satires in the 1720s and '30s. But Fielding was not as partisan as his contemporaries. His broader target was the hypocrisy of the rich and well-to-do, as well as all that was asinine in eighteenth-century culture. His motives were a mixture of authentic disgust at the lack of moral accountability amongst the gentry and a more mercenary commercial imperative to make money in a theatrical marketplace where anti-government satire was becoming one of the more prominent genres. Nevertheless, it was Fielding who became synonymous with 'Walpole bashing' in the first minister's eyes.

Henry Fielding. (*Mysteries of Police & Crime*, Vol. I, Cassell and Company Ltd, first published 1898)

Henry Fielding was born in Sharpton Park, Somerset, to a wealthy and connected family, but complications with his inheritance meant that he was a relatively poor man when he entered London. He had an abortive career in the law and a botched elopement behind him. There was a need to establish his reputation quickly and make money. He turned to the theatre.

Fielding's theatrical career began inauspiciously in 1728 with *Love in Several Masques*, staged at Drury Lane. It was a comedy seen as imitative of the Restoration playwright William Congreve. It had little impact but Fielding was remarkably prolific, producing twenty-five theatrical works in nine years, the content of which became increasingly satiric and troublesome. In 1830 Fielding penned *Tom Thumb*, an absurdist parody of the sort of Heroic Tragedies popular at the time. The work was successful and ran for forty nights. A year later he wrote *The Welsh Opera* (later revised and retitled *The Grub Street Opera*). Once again, the work was staged at Drury Lane. It owed a debt to *The Beggar's Opera* in its choice of dramatic form (the ballad opera) and in some of its targets. The story was set in a household where servants stole from their masters. The masters doubled for the royal family, and the servants for Walpole and William Pulteney, the opposition leader. In a sense the satire was fairly even-handed, rubbishing both sides. Fielding had not yet made a significant enemy out of Walpole and his animosity was not yet a given, the playwright even dedicating one of his next works to Walpole.

Fielding's *The Author's Farce* (1730) reverted back to mocking Walpole, but the first minister had received harsher savaging from more vitriolic wits. Fielding was not yet a ruthless satirist. He would graduate to the top rank of Walpole's tormenters with the staging of the provocatively titled *Rape Upon Rape; or The Justice Caught In His Own Trap.*

Rape Upon Rape drew on Walpole's perceived involvement in a vile criminal episode involving a well-connected ally of the government. Colonel Francis Charteris was a disgraced soldier and gambler. He was also a runner for Walpole. On top of all that, Charteris was an insatiable womaniser and was known to employ attractive women as servants in order to seduce them. He was generally successful in his pursuit of sex but on one occasion was turned down by Anna Bond, his housemaid. Charteris was incensed; he beat and raped her. She brought a prosecution against him and he was convicted and committed to Newgate. By rite he should have been hanged, but Charteris paid a large amount of money to friends in the government and was spared the gallows, pardoned by the king and set free. The decision provoked outrage and disgust. When Charteris died of syphilis shortly afterwards his open grave was pelted with dead animals by an angry mob. There was a rough poetic justice to his death, but the manner of his exit did nothing to stop the belief of the populace that the law existed to protect the rich.

Charteris was still alive when *Rape Upon Rape* was performed, but he was not the principal target of the satire. Although nobody could (or ever would) prove it, Walpole was believed to have used his influence with the king to secure Charteris' pardon. This set of circumstances brought out a more vicious quality in Henry Fielding's writing. This time the Walpole substitute was a dishonest justice named Squeezum. It was the most personal portrait from the author yet, and the thick-skinned, frequently scorned first minister was believed at last to have taken issue with Fielding.

In 1737 Fielding wrote *The Historical Register for 1736* and satirised Walpole not once, but twice during the same evening's entertainment. The first sideswipe appeared in the guise of Quidam, one of five useless and corrupt politicians. The second Walpole doppelganger took the form of the character Pillage, a playhouse manager who papers his own theatre's auditorium with sycophants and cronies in order to assure his own play's success. Quidam and Pillage were both deeply insulting versions of Walpole and the play was a well-received work that came at the end of a successful run that established Fielding as second only to Colley Cibber as the most popular dramatist in the country.

Walpole's response was to instigate the drafting of a Licensing Bill that would regulate the production of theatrical performances. But Walpole had to tread carefully; for his part, the bill could not be seen as born out of a sense of personal effrontery. Walpole had to demonstrate that suppressing the form of satire that he was routinely subject to was in the nation's best interests rather than his own. An anonymous play entitled *The Golden Rump* provided him with all the ammunition he needed to move against Fielding and his ilk.

'The Festival of the Golden Rump' was originally a print that depicted the king as a satyr. The king in the form of half-man, half-goat thrusts his royal anus at the queen, while a robed priest or magician bearing an uncanny resemblance to Walpole looks on approvingly. *The Golden Rump* was a theatrical adaptation of the print. It was in circulation but had not as yet been performed on the stage. The staging of such a work would have been incendiary, and as the royal family were being more brutally satirised than Walpole, the first minister had the perfect platform from which to push through personally advantageous legislation under the guise of protecting royal dignity.

The playright of *The Golden Rump* remains a mystery to this day. Fielding was naturally touted as a possibility. The ferocious Jacobite, William King, was another probable suspect. Fielding even claimed that Walpole had privately set the whole episode in motion, with *The Golden Rump* being written specifically to provide a context for the new bill.

The bill set out harsh and restrictive terms by which plays could be staged. No theatre could operate without a royal patent. Any theatrical work wishing to see the light of day had to be presented first to the Lord Chamberlain a fortnight before it was to be performed. If the Lord Chamberlain deemed the content inappropriate, the work would not be performed. The consequences for disobeying the act could be brutal, whipping being one of the penalties that could be implemented for anyone who defied it. The bill was fast-tracked through Parliament unopposed by everyone except the Earl of Chesterfield, who gave a beautiful speech that was well received but completely ignored, as the majority voted in Walpole's favour and the bill became law.

With the Act passed, Walpole settled some longstanding debts. Lincoln's Inn Fields was closed and when John Gay wrote *Polly*, a sequel to *The Beggar's Opera*, the Licensing Act was invoked to ensure that it wasn't performed. Henry Fielding's career was over. Under the conditions laid out by the Act, Walpole's administration would never permit Fielding to operate as a playwright. As far as the theatre was concerned, he had been effectively silenced. After dabbling in journalism and the law for a season, Fielding turned to the novel. He found the form that would best suit his formidable gifts and began to build his reputation as one of the truly great writers of the century. He wrote *An Apology for the Life of Mrs Shamela Andrews* (1741) and *The Adventures of Joseph Harrison* (1742) as a means of sending up the prose of his new target, the popular novelist Samuel Richardson; but for his third novel Fielding invoked the ghost of Jonathan Wild for one last battle with the first minister.

The Life of Mr. Jonathan Wild the Great originally appeared in 1743 as the third part of Fielding's *Miscellanies*. Volume one consisted of poetry; volume two contained plays and an unfinished work, *From This World to the Next*; and volume three was mostly taken up with Jonathan Wild. Unlike Defoe, Fielding had no real interest in precisely replicating the details and methodology of the Thief Taker General's life and career, or trying to understand the moral and social anomaly that was Wild and his organisation. Fielding mischievously plays fast and loose with the facts of his life. Wild is still a successful receiver of stolen goods and his criminal techniques are accurately depicted. Wild's laudanum overdose and the hostile reception at his hanging are present and correct. Blueskin Blake still assaults Wild but stabs him in the guts in an argument over a stolen watch rather than slashing his throat. Roger Johnson makes an appearance but as a rival in a power struggle with Wild over which of them holds sway over the prisoners of Newgate, but Jack Sheppard is conspicuous by his absence.

The plot is mainly concerned with Wild's attempts to swindle his friend Heartfree and then frame him for the loss of his own fortune, all the while trying to seduce (or when that fails, molest) Heartfree's virtuous wife. The plotting is outrageous and entertaining, but what gives the work its edge is the ironic commentary on the notion of greatness. *Jonathan Wild the Great* exists in a topsy-turvy moral universe where the narrator assumes all mankind is callous and grasping, and that unalloyed virtue places its practitioner at the bottom of the food chain and is therefore a ridiculous and unnatural state of being. The distinction is made between greatness and goodness, the road to greatness being a naturally selfish and ruthless one. The word 'great' is invoked again and again, and multiple allusions are made between Wild's criminal practices and those of other respectable, so-called great men:

> Indeed, whoever considers the common fate of great men must allow that they well deserve and hardly earn the applause which is given them by the world; for, when we reflect on the labours and pains, the cares, disquietudes, and dangers which attend their road to greatness, we may say with the divine that a man may go to heaven with half the pains it cost him to purchase hell.

Ultimately, Wild is hanged and Mr and Mrs Heartfree are reunited and their fortune restored, but the aftertaste of the comic viciousness of the Fielding/ Wild universe remains.

Of course, one of Walpole's frequent nicknames was The Great Man, and the parallels in Fielding's novel between crime and the machinery of politics at work were obvious to any reader at the time. But *Jonathan Wild the Great* is a strange work for so sharp and topical a satirist. Fielding's timing was off. By the time *Jonathan Wild the Great* was published, Walpole was finished. The first minister had been uncharacteristically manoeuvred, against his own political instincts, into war with Spain. The war went badly and at last Walpole's power base crumbled. He was now a redundant target for satirists. Also, Jonathan Wild had been dead for almost two decades and would have seemed a stale choice as a satiric weapon. Theories abound as to why Fielding wrote the novel at all. Some believe that his target was not so much Walpole as a more general swipe at hypocrisy. Some think that Walpole's contemporary (and main beneficiary of the first minister's downfall), William Pulteney, was the target. The most resonant theory seems to be that Fielding wrote *Jonathan Wild* in 1740, when Walpole was teetering on the brink of ruin but still something of a force to be reckoned with, and that the sections that seem to criticise Walpole's successors were added later. Nobody knows for certain, but whatever the questions of timing or satiric political relevance, the novel has endured whereas Fielding's plays are seldom, if ever, performed today.

Fielding's most enduring work, the novel *Tom Jones*, was still to come. He also served a historic tenure as a magistrate that would help establish the foundations for much of modern policing.[1] Jonathan Wild had been re-injected into the imaginations of English readers and the literary notion of corporate master villainy was kept alive. But Wild's independent opposite had not been idle. Jack Sheppard's legacy was preserved in the paintings and engravings of two highly prominent artists.

THORNHILL

In November 1724 an austere gentleman visited Newgate and paid his 1s 6d to gain access to the heavily manacled Jack Sheppard. He had brought drawing materials with him and sketched the outlaw. He returned to the studio and painted what he had drawn. A month later, prints of the portrait were being sold for 1s.

The portrait showed Sheppard unadorned and in chains assuming something close to a suppliant's pose. The image has been praised for showing a criminal phenomenon shorn of the trappings of his celebrity; a human being confronting the sober reality of his impending execution. The exact same image has also been criticised for eulogising the thief, giving him the more laudable stance of someone about to die for a worthy cause. Ambiguity surrounds the painting, most notably because of its originator. The artist was Sir James Thornhill and his portrait of Jack Sheppard was a complete anomaly in his large, impressive, conservative body of work.

Sir James Thornhill's portrait of Jack Sheppard.

Thornhill was the epitome of all that was currently fashionable and tasteful in the Georgian art world. He had studied under Thomas Highmore and specialised in decorative painting. Decorative art used the interior walls or roof of a grand building as a canvas and incorporated the architecture into the (often mythologically themed) painting that adorned it, giving the art an added sense of physical depth and dimension. It was a genre hugely popular on the Continent. Its popularity naturally extended to England but its specialists were largely foreign until Thornhill perfected the style and became its great English practitioner.

Thornhill's roster of commissions and laurels was extraordinary. Prior to his Newgate visit he had created decorative works at Blenheim, Hampton Court, Moor Park and St Paul's Cathedral. His portrait of Sheppard was painted during a hiatus from his great work in progress, the decoration of the anteroom and upper and lower halls of Greenwich Naval Hospital. By 1724 Thornhill was History Painter in Ordinary to the king and ran his own painting academy. In fact, Thornhill upheld the artistic status quo on so many levels that his portrait of a famous thief is all the more conspicuous.

In much the same way that an accurate interpretation of the portrait's meaning still invites discussion, the exact reason for Thornhill creating it in the first place is still a source of head-scratching and chin-rubbing centuries later. Thornhill's sketchpad is often at odds with his official output and was

peppered with etchings of rougher characters than ever appeared in his commissioned works. There was certainly a part of the artist that enjoyed a degree
of association with the seedier elements of London society, as Thornhill could
frequently be spotted drinking in Covent Garden pubs. But that kind of personal duality could have been laid at the feet of many of the most prominent
Georgian figures.

His motives for painting Sheppard have been ascribed to a singular attempt
to acknowledge (and have a taste of) the sensationalistic art market emerging
among the middle classes, or else a one-off commercial indulgence of his
private artistic tastes. The truth is that no one knows. But the incontestable
factor is that of the irresistible spell Jack Sheppard cast over all quarters of
Georgian society and particularly the creative community. The mantle would
be taken up by one of the great artistic pioneers of the age, William Hogarth,
and Sheppard's shadow would cast and recast itself in various forms around
his work throughout his life.

HOGARTH

Hogarth was Thornhill's son-in-law and may well have been present with
him at Newgate when he sketched Sheppard. Hogarth's professional fascination with London's underworld was not anomalous like Thornhill's was.
Hogarth would return again and again to the capital's thieves, rakes, prostitutes and murderers in an extraordinary and unprecedented series of works
that would eclipse in reputation, originality and influence anything else he
would accomplish as an artist.

Hogarth's personal association with the world he would illustrate so vividly
started early, and was not of his own choosing. In 1703 Hogarth's father had
been locked up for debt. He was a Latin scholar whose business enterprise
(a coffee house) had gone bust, confining him to the Fleet Gaol. Hogarth's
father languished in prison until 1712, when an Act of Parliament freed all
debtors who owed £50 or less. In 1713 poverty necessitated that Hogarth
apprentice himself to Ellis Gamble, a silver engraver; Hogarth was 17 years
old. Five years later his father was dead, and two years after that Hogarth
had completed his apprenticeship and had gone into business for himself. His
output was varied, including shop cards and play tickets. He also produced
the odd work of satire. The commercial imperatives of earning a living ran
concurrent with his attempts to develop as an artist. Hogarth enrolled in St
Martin's Lane Academy until it closed in 1724. That same year Hogarth took
up his studies at James Thornhill's Academy in Covent Garden and it was
around this time Hogarth produced his first notable satire; the subject was the

South Sea Crises. Soon afterwards, Jack Sheppard provided the pretext upon which William Hogarth launched a stinging attack on the theatrical world.

Sheppard's body had hardly stiffened in the grave when a pantomime was staged at the Drury Lane Theatre mythologising his achievements. *Harlequin Sheppard* was produced by Gay and Fielding's rival and enemy, Colly Cibber. Hogarth was generally enraptured by the theatre but took violent issue with this production. The Drury Lane company's manifesto had been to provide elevated art for the London theatre-going public. This was a laudable principle but it was practised only until commercial jealousy over John Gay's more seemingly populist output obliged them to lower their sights and produce entertainments like the Sheppard pantomime. This was a crass double standard in Hogarth's eyes and demanded a response. His repost was blunt to say the least. *A Just View from the British Stage, or, Three Heads are Better than One* was a print packed with insulting detail. The 'Three Heads' were Colly Cibber and his co-managers Barton Booth and Robert Wilkes. The print depicted a rehearsal of *Harlequin Sheppard*, but the central image was that of the spectre of the great Tudor and Jacobean playwright, Ben Johnson, emerging from a trapdoor and registering his disapproval at what was going on around him by pissing all over a heap of theatrical props.

Of course, the next great Sheppard-inflected work was *The Beggar's Opera*. John Gay's opus inspired Hogarth and the consequence was a far subtler and enduring work of art. *The Beggar's Opera* paintings were Hogarth's first great works in oils. He painted around half a dozen variations of the same scene. The central image is Macheath in chains in the Lincoln's Inn Fields facsimile of Newgate Gaol, with Lucy Locket and Polly Peachum either side of him, begging their respective fathers to spare the highwayman's life. To the far right and left of the main characters are the more notable and affluent members of the theatre audience, sitting, according to the theatrical conventions of the time, onstage with the cast. The paintings broke new ground. They are believed to be some of the first paintings to show an actual English theatrical performance.

Hogarth was not so interested in the drama unfolding on stage, or the satiric properties of Macheath and Peachum, Sheppard and Wild, as in the multi-layered social dynamics of the audience and the actors that they had come to see. The vibrant inner life of a performance was Hogarth's real subject, as high and low society collided and colluded against the backdrop of a London stage performance. With each successive version of the painting the audience become more and more prominent. By the final image the most compelling narrative element is not the performance of the play, but rather the covert interplay between the actress playing Polly Peachum and an adoring aristocrat in the audience (this reflected the real-life scandal that was playing out during *The Beggar's Opera*'s long run, as the Duke of Bolton and the actress Lavinia

Fenton conducted an affair that would culminate in a disreputable marriage).
In working and reworking the scene, Hogarth was toying with ideas that he
would come back to and fully develop in a genre of his own devising. It
was a genre that would secure Hogarth's reputation as a pioneering artist and
social documentarian. And in one of his greatest works the influence of Jack
Sheppard would be much in evidence.

In 1730 Hogarth painted a picture of a prostitute getting out of bed. The
painting became something of a talking point amongst visitors to Hogarth's
studio and he was encouraged to paint a sequel. Hogarth ended up painting
three sequels and two prequels. In the series of six images Hogarth told the
story of a naive country girl's arrival in London and her induction into the
world of prostitution, her brief period of affluence as a courtesan and her
rapid decline in health and fortune culminating in a spell in the Bridewell and
a degrading death from venereal disease. Amongst the picture's roster of supporting characters, Hogarth included a smattering of recognisable underworld
figures. In the first image, the young girl is procured by Mother Needham (a
notorious London madam), while the rapist, Colonel Charteris, and his toady
and pimp, John Gourly, look on lecherously from the sidelines. There is even
a tilted nod to the legacy of Jack Sheppard in the inclusion of a picture of
Macheath above the whore's bed.

The images presented a cautionary tale on the respective evils and perils
of prostitution, but also stood as an indictment of a hypocritical society that
permitted (and even subtly encouraged) prostitution to thrive, whilst brutally punishing and abandoning its most vulnerable practitioners. The series of
fiercely moralistic images came to be known as *The Harlot's Progress*. Hogarth
had created something new and would capitalise on his innovation.

In 1732 Hogarth made engravings of *The Harlot's Progress* and charged a
guinea for each set. It was a shrewd financial move and, despite a flurry of
pirated versions, Hogarth did very well. Hogarth the artist, moralist, satirist
and businessman had found the form that would define him for the rest of
his life. Despite digressions into the realms of portrait-painting and Biblical
art, it was the Moral Progress that Hogarth returned to time and time again
whenever he felt the need to expose the endemic double standards, in all
their multifarious forms, rotting the heart of Georgian society. *The Harlot's
Progress* found its mirror image in *The Rake's Progress*, arranged marriages were
criticised in *Marriage a-la-Mode*, the relationship between sadism in children
and criminality in adults in *The Four Stages of Cruelty*, and corrupt election
practices were lampooned in *The Election Entertainment*.

Industry and Idleness was a particularly lengthy Moral Progress that depicted
the concurrent paths of two apprentices, one lazy and one hardworking.
Naturally, the conscientious apprentice (Francis Goodchild) is promoted,

Tom Idle is hanged at Tyburn in part 11 of Hogarth's moral progress, *Industry and Idleness*. Tom Idle is believed to have been based on Jack Sheppard.

marries the boss's daughter and assumes a place of prominence in society as a magistrate. The lazy apprentice (Tom Idle) spends his earnings and his energy on gambling and prostitution. He drifts easily into a life of crime and is eventually implicated in a murder. He is betrayed by his lover (a whore), tried and reluctantly sentenced to death by none other than Francis Goodchild. The moral may not be subtle,[2] but the brilliance of the work is in the frenzied, detailed, almost apocalyptic rendering of Tom Idle's descent. And the inspiration for Tom Idle is believed by many to be Jack Sheppard. Historian Lucy Moore suggests that Tom Idle's features were lifted from Thornhill's portrait, and points to parallels between Sheppard's life and Tom Idle's story. Hogarth biographer Jenny Uglow sees Tom Idle's story as being inflected with the same fugitive romance that had flavoured people's memory of the real Jack Sheppard. Certainly, in the following century, Victorians regarded Sheppard as the inspiration for Tom Idle. One of the most popular fictional works on the outlaw contained a chapter entitled 'The Idle Apprentice'. And if that was too subtle an allusion for Victorian readers then the writer staged a scene in which Thornhill, Hogarth and John Gay meet the condemned prisoner who simultaneously inspires them to paint his portrait, write *The Beggar's Opera* and create *The Idle Apprentice*. The book was *Jack Sheppard, A Romance*. The author was William Harrison Ainsworth.

Sheppard and Wild had been spoiled. Their legacy had been well served by many of the best artistic figures of the eighteenth century. It was only fair that a bad Victorian writer should have a go.

WILLIAM HARRISON AINSWORTH

For about half a decade William Harrison Ainsworth was perhaps the most commercially successful author in the country. He was attractive, youthful and wealthy. He was the social centre of the London literary scene and a great benefactor, acting as something of a mentor to the young Charles Dickens. Originally from Manchester, Ainsworth's family were rich, his father having made a fortune in surveying. Ainsworth tried his hand at law. When his father died, Ainsworth was only 19 years old and was expected to take his place at the head of the firm. Ainsworth was not a natural lawyer and quickly found himself in over his head, so much so that it was deemed necessary to send him to London to get more training. Yet Ainsworth became a writer instead. If his father had wanted him to continue in his own footsteps then he would have to have taken a degree of responsibility for the direction his son subsequently took. Father and son's relationship had been a good one. Ainsworth senior had been a consummate storyteller it seemed, fuelling in his child a love of local myth and outlaw narratives, specifically tales of highwaymen. Ainsworth's adult imagination teemed with the same influences that had stimulated it as a child, with one important addition; he was a devotee of the Gothic Romance.

As a genre, Gothic Romance had come to prominence in the second half of the eighteenth century. Gothic Romance as a literary form revelled in melodramatic scenarios played out within the geographical confines of storm-blasted castles and monasteries. Gothic stories were often supernatural. The setting was invariably medieval Italy. The weather was stormy; the light was shadow; the villains were either counts or monks.

Ainsworth also loved the Historical Romance as practised by Sir Walter Scott. It was in the latter genre that Ainsworth's first novel, *Sir John Chiverton*, appeared in 1826. *Sir John Chiverton*, despite earning a nod of approbation from Sir Walter himself, was a modest success. In 1834 Ainsworth took elements of Historical Romance and baptised them in unconstrained Gothic sensibilities transposed to an English idyll. The result was the novel *Rookwood*.

Rookwood had its creative genesis in a trip to Chesterfield, when Ainsworth was walking through the graveyard of St Mary's, Chesterfield's famous church with the twisted spire. A tomb was being opened and Ainsworth watched with interest. The event imprinted itself on his imagination and a story began to take form. He did a little work on his new idea in Chesterfield and then abandoned it for a year. A visit to Cuckfield Place, an Elizabethan House in Sussex, was the impetus Ainsworth needed to re-fire his imagination and resume his story.

Rookwood wove the tale of the historical highwayman Dick Turpin into a Gothic universe of family curses, secrets, murder and old dark houses.

Rookwood was published in three volumes in 1834. And although technically, Ainsworth's Turpin was a supporting character and subsidiary to the Gothic contrivances at the centre of the narrative, he dominated the novel. The Victorian public rediscovered an old villain and embraced him as a folk hero. Turpin had not been forgotten exactly but Ainsworth succeeded in fixing a version of him in the English imagination that still persists today. And if there had previously been any ambivalence about the thief, Ainsworth did much to erase that, taking a ruthless criminal and refashioning him as a roguish but essentially honourable Robin Hood figure. Ainsworth even introduced elements of the Turpin story that are often taken as fact today (Black Bess, the name given to Dick Turpin's preternaturally fast horse, being a complete Ainsworth contrivance).

St Mary's Church where William Harrison Ainsworth had his literary epiphany. (Mark Nightingale)

After witnessing a tomb being opened in St Mary's cemetery, Ainsworth was inspired to write his Dick Turpin novel *Rookwood*. (Mark Nightingale)

Rookwood was immensely successful. Many bad reviews, as well as moral concerns regarding the level of hero worship accorded to Ainsworth's Turpin, did nothing to stem the pace with which copies were bought. By 1837 *Rookwood* was in its 6th edition, had been adapted for the stage and inspired seemingly endless Turpin-themed Penny Dreadfuls, emulating the style and content of Ainsworth's work.

Ainsworth followed *Rookwood* with *Crighton*, the tale of a Scotsman in the Court of Henri III, King of France. It was a throwback to the type of fiction he had been writing before *Rookwood*. *Crighton* was not a great success. Ainsworth returned to the formula that had made him famous and in 1839 a new tale, centred this time on Jack Sheppard, began to appear in serial form. The series was so successful that the novel version was rushed into publication even before the serial had finished its run. Ainsworth's *Jack Sheppard* was published in the same year as Dickens' *Oliver Twist* and outsold it.

JACK SHEPPARD: A ROMANCE

Ainsworth's novel walks a strange tightrope between historical fidelity and gruesome fairy tale. He systematically ticks off every important Jack Sheppard escapade. Most of the characters in the Sheppard/Wild narrative are present, and Ainsworth's descriptions of Newgate have the forensic integrity of a man who had actually visited the prison in the course of his research. In the early stages of the story Ainsworth's cheerfully impish Sheppard is historically recognisable. But the narrative spine of the novel is a preposterous tale of two foundling cousins (one of whom turns out to be Sheppard) who unbeknown to them are related to a motley collection of disgraced, dead or dying aristocrats. The cousins try to evade the evil designs of a corrupt relative in league with a thoroughly demonic Jonathan Wild.

The plot rotates on a series of outrageous coincidences. The dialogue is generally awful. The novel is appallingly anti-Semitic in its presentation of Abraham Mendez and equally racist in its depiction of a minor black character named Caliban. And while Ainsworth faithfully recreates the majority of Sheppard's exploits, he puts an unintentional comic spin on most of them. Much of this is down to the moral U-turn that Jack Sheppard undergoes when he is accidentally complicit in the murder of a benefactor's widow. From that point on, Sheppard becomes a penitent crusader against Wild and his cohorts, and whenever Sheppard is caught by Wild, it is usually because he has deliberately placed himself in danger by dint of doing something honourable rather than the stupidity or treachery that preceded most of Jack Sheppard's actual arrests. Sheppard ultimately sacrifices himself to the gallows in the process of establishing his cousin's aristocratic lineage. Ainsworth doesn't permit Sheppard to live, but spares him the agony of the noose when soldiers shoot him dead on the gallows during a noble but botched escape attempt organised by Blueskin Blake. Wild lives, but his house is burnt down by the London mob, his throat has been slashed and his henchmen are dead; similarly, Quilt Arnold is shot through the head and Abraham Mendez lynched. Before he dies, Jack Sheppard prophesies that within a year Wild will hang.

On so many levels Ainsworth's novel is appalling, but it does have an almost schizophrenic quality that allows lines like, 'It was a night of storm and terror, which promised each moment to become more stormy and more terrible', to coexist with, 'It's a miserable weakness to be afraid of bloodshed – The general who gives an order for wholesale carnage never sleeps a wink the less soundly for the midnight groans of his victims ...' The decently written latter example is a speech given by Wild and it is in his depiction of villainy and the wholesale embracing of the Gothic principles of atmosphere, architecture and violent incident that Ainsworth triumphs. The heroes in the novel (including a post-repentance Sheppard) are likeable but dull. The villains have more vigour but are still grotesque. Wild's villainy is underscored in a rather pedantic manner as he is described repeatedly in diabolical terms. Wild has a 'Satanic grin', 'the grin of a fiend', a 'diabolical grin'. Wild doesn't have teeth

In *Jack Sheppard*, Jonathan Wild fishes a severed head out of the waters of the Thames, beneath London Bridge at night. (*Three Hundred and Sixty-Five Views of London*, Rock Bros Ltd)

so much as 'fangs to the farthest extremity of his mouth'. Yet Ainsworth is at his absolute best when describing something unpleasant happening in a labyrinthine house or prison. Sinister buildings are the real characters in Ainsworth's prose. Wild's home becomes a gothic lair with secret passageways and a private museum of curiosities containing the skulls of executed murderers. Ainsworth extends this command of Gothic style to his depiction of a weather-beaten and mouldy Georgian London, skilfully mixing horror and geography. At one point Wild, on a skiff on the Thames, is distracted by something bobbing in the water:

> It proved to be a human head, though with scarcely a vestige of the features remaining. Here and there, patches of flesh adhered to the bones, and the dank dripping hair hanging about what had once been the face, gave it a ghastly appearance.
>
> 'It's the skull of a rebel,' said Jonathan, with marked emphasis on the word, 'blown by the wind from a spike on the bridge above us. I don't know whose brainless head it may be, but it'll do for my collection.' And he tossed it carelessly into the bottom of the boat.

It is numerous sequences like this that give the book a vigour that balances the more problematic questions of style, tone and cavalier plotting, making *Jack Sheppard* a thrilling read almost in spite of itself.

If *Rookwood* had conjoined the Gothic and the Historical Romance, then *Jack Sheppard* married the Gothic Romance to another popular genre that had emerged in the 1830s. Newgate Fictions were crime narratives culled in the main from the *Newgate Calendar*, the pre-eminent and perpetually updated chronicle of the most notorious British criminals from 1700 to the time of publication. London went berserk for the Georgian thief. Like *Rookwood* before it, *Jack Sheppard* was a huge commercial success. And like *Rookwood*, *Jack Sheppard* prompted numerous stage adaptations, seven of which opened within a month of the novel appearing on the bookshelves; one theatre even sold Sheppard merchandise in the form of burglary kits. Unsurprisingly, the critical response was mostly negative and the same moral concerns resurfaced about Sheppard's corrupting properties on Victorian youth that had beset *Rookwood*. The levels of moral concern were more intense surrounding *Jack Sheppard* than *Rookwood*, and for a brief moment it looked like Ainsworth's critics were justified when the worlds of authentic criminality and Newgate Fiction blurred into one another for a brief moment.

COURVOISIER & THE DECLINE OF WILLIAM AINSWORTH

Less than a year after the publication of *Jack Sheppard*, Francois Benjamin Courvoisier, a Swiss valet, was arrested for the murder of his employer. Courvoisier worked for Lord William Russell, who he had been stealing from. Courvoisier's thefts had been frequent and Lord Russell had begun to harbour suspicions, so Courvoisier decided to kill him. On 3 May 1840 Lord Russell was at his club. He returned home around midnight and went to bed, whereupon Courvoisier visited him in his bedroom and cut his throat. He then set about the room trying to make it look as if burglars had broken in and had committed the murder.

Servants discovered Russell's body the following morning and Courvoisier's attempts to screen his own guilt were unsuccessful. He was arrested and put on trial, convicted and sentenced to hang. Thirty thousand people attended his execution; Dickens and Thackery were both there, as well as a conspicuous number of servants in the crowd. The trial and hanging was for a while the great cause célèbre in the capital.

Courvoisier had privately admitted guilt to his defence lawyer but publically he blamed others for his crime. Initially, Courvoisier pointed the finger at his fellow servants. When the credibility of that line of defence collapsed and Courvoisier's guilt was established, the valet looked for another scapegoat and blamed William Harrison Ainsworth. Courvoisier claimed that he had

Murder victim Lord William
Russell's snuffbox. (Object
courtesy of The Galleries of
Justice, Nottingham; photographed
by Mark Nightingale)

(Inset) A closer examination reveals
Lord Russell's bloodstains still
visible on the snuffbox. (Object
courtesy of The Galleries of
Justice, Nottingham; photographed
by Mark Nightingale)

been reading *Jack Sheppard* prior to the killing. He stated that Ainsworth's
book had prompted him to murder his employer.

Apart from more unwelcome moralising and the shutting down of one
of the Sheppard plays (which Ainsworth made no money from anyway), the
Courvoisier scandal did little to arrest *Jack Sheppard*'s commercial momentum.
Ainsworth was at his zenith. But the popularity of his works would not out-
live him. What eventually destroyed him commercially and critically were the
rapid shifts in taste and the changing fashions in literature towards authenticity. The next stage in the literary evolution of Newgate Fiction was realism.
Although *Jack Sheppard* had outsold *Oliver Twist*, it was Dickens' commitment
to a de-sanitised, unglamorous depiction of the underworld that commanded

readers' attention from that point on. Ainsworth had to suffer the indignity of seeing what had once been considered an incendiary duo of novels, become 'quaint' and 'passé' in his own lifetime. He carried on writing into old age, but his fortunes and celebrity diminished in proportion to Dickens, his onetime protégé's ascendancy.

In a way, Ainsworth had returned Sheppard and Wild to the narrative purity of their original dispute. Ainsworth's Wild and Sheppard had no satiric properties to speak of. They were simply a villain and an anti-hero perpetuating a vendetta that had been raging in one form or another for over a century.

A HOLMESIAN INTERLUDE

Sheppard would be dormant for a while, but towards the end of the century Jonathan Wild was famously name-checked by Arthur Conan Doyle when Professor Moriarty, the evil foil to Doyle's great master detective Sherlock Holmes, made his first chronological appearance in *The Valley of Fear*. The novel was written after Moriarty's initial appearance in print but set prior to the events of his debut in the short story *The Final Problem*. In *The Valley of Fear*, Holmes, trying to explain to a sceptical police inspector who Moriarty is and how he operates, cites Jonathan Wild as a historical precedent. This is one of the most famous references to Wild in crime fiction, yet there seems to be another, more oblique reference to him in *The Final Problem*. Holmes is having more or less the same conversation with his companion Dr Watson that he had had with Inspector MacDonald in *The Valley of Fear*. As Watson is more intelligent and more sympathetic to Holmes designs than Inspector MacDonald, Holmes is more effusive. In describing Moriarty he makes an allusion to another tyrannical historical figure:

> He is the Napoleon of crime, Watson. He is the organiser of half that is evil and nearly all that is undetected in this great city. He is a genius, a philosopher, an abstract thinker. He has a brain of the first order. He sits motionless, like a spider in the centre of its web, but that web has a thousand radiations, and he knows well every quiver of each of them.

In *Jack Sheppard* this is how Ainsworth describes Jonathan Wild: 'He was the Napoleon of knavery, and established an uncontrolled empire over all the practitioners of crime.' It seemed that Doyle had read Ainsworth, and had Ainsworth's version of Wild in mind when he created Moriarty, perhaps even slightly plagiarising Ainsworth in the famous allusion to Napoleon that Wild and Moriarty both shared.[3]

SHEPPARD & WILD, A WEIMAR POSTSCRIPT

Although the great feud was almost at an end, Wild and Sheppard were not entirely forgotten, and neither were they completely finished with each other. They would leave London, assume tried and tested pseudonyms, and resume hostilities in the theatres of Weimar Germany. In the 1930s Berthold Brecht and Kurt Weil reinvented *The Beggar's Opera* in the form of its bastard cousin, *The Threepenny Opera*. Peachum and Macheath were resurrected, the London setting was retained but the story was transposed to the nineteenth century. A single song was taken from John Gay's original. The rest of the music was an innovative and strange mix comprising elements of tango, carnival, choral and jazz in an ugly-beautiful collision of discordant styles and unsettling rhythms. This time the underworld was intended to substitute itself for the German bourgeoisie in its various compromised forms. As a piece of satire, *The Threepenny Opera* proved to be an unusually fudged and indistinct work in terms of what its exact political point was. But what *The Threepenny Opera* lacked in political coherence was immaterial when laid against the brilliance of the world Brecht and Weil created, the characters that inhabited that world, the gutter poetry they spoke and sang, and the music that accompanied it. *The Threepenny Opera* transcended the rather didactic intentions of its creators to become something more universal. The public loved it, the Nazis hated it and when Hitler assumed power, *The Threepenny Opera*'s blend of decadence and perceived Bolshevik propaganda had its authors fleeing for their lives.

As a work only superficially rooted in London life and its criminal tradition, it is not the purpose of this chapter to explore in detail the fascinating genesis and afterlife of this extraordinary piece of theatre, suffice to say that *The Threepenny Opera* would be the last truly great work to date attributable to the colourful and endlessly adaptable examples of Jonathan Wild and Jack Sheppard.[4]

PART TWO:

SUNDRY MASTER VILLAINS & ONE VILLAINESS

3

A Notorious Baggage

Comedy & Tragedy

Dramatising outrageous criminality was one of the great narrative staples of the expansive and popular theatrical scene of late sixteenth- and early seventeenth-century London. From the first performances of Thomas Kyd's feverish and gory *The Spanish Tragedy* to John Webster's duo of dark and poetic works *The White Devil* and *The Duchess of Malfi*, the public taste for murder answered by bloody revenge was consistent and frequently rewarded with outstanding theatre. But the serious dramatisation of crime in Tudor and Jacobean theatre preferred a European setting (preferably Spanish or Italian), or else plundered English history or Roman and Greek antiquity for its inspiration. An aristocratic context was also obligatory for any tragedy worth its salt. Directly reflecting the worlds of the majority of the audiences who came to see these productions was not the concern of the tragedian. Yet Tudor and Jacobean London was a city with an increasingly sophisticated criminal underworld that produced its fair share of noteworthy crimes and flamboyant criminal personalities. Save for a couple of exceptions, contemporary indigenous crime, as experienced by the majority of the London populous, had no place in English tragedy. Comedy was another matter. London life and its overlap with criminal society, and the often inept and corrupt powers of law enforcement that tried to control it, was the backdrop of many popular and bawdy plays of the era. And the life of the most extraordinary of all sixteenth- and early seventeenth-century master criminals collided with the concerns and imaginations of the two playwrights most associated with dramatising London life. The criminal was Moll Cutpurse and the playwrights were Thomas Middleton and Thomas Dekker.

MOLL CUTPURSE

Moll Cutpurse was a visible fixture of Holborn, Fleet Street and St Paul's. She was difficult to miss as she dressed in men's clothing, wore a sword, was probably very tall and smoked a pipe. If you didn't see her you were likely to hear her as she had a reputation for loud boisterous behaviour and swore profusely and fluently. She was considered physically formidable and very good with a sword, a staff, a pistol, and when necessary her fists. Opinions differed as to whether she was attractive or ugly. Her area of criminal endeavour was theft and the receiving of stolen goods. She was believed to have run a shop in Fleet Street where stolen items were brought to her, immediately displayed in her shop window and then sold back to their original owners. Her reputation among the criminal community seemed to be one of fairness.

The facts and legend of Moll Cutpurse's life are so intermingled that they make any kind of accurate biography nigh on impossible. There are one or two instances in her long and strange life that seem incontestable, the rest is a mixture of conjecture and myth making. Her real name was Mary Frith. The consensus seems to be that she was born in 1584. The stories surrounding her early life and induction into crime go something like this:

Mary Frith, also known as Moll Cutpurse.

Fleet Street. Mary Frith was a visible fixture of Jacobean Fleet Street. (*Three Hundred and Sixty-Five Views of London*, Rock Bros Ltd)

She was raised in Aldersgate near St Paul's. Her father was a shoemaker. She had a wild streak from an early age and was the source of much vexation to her parents. To their credit they tried to ensure that she received some formal education, but their ambitions for her didn't seem to extend much beyond a good marriage. Mary Frith abhorred the notion of marriage, preferring the company of boys to girls, which often extended to fist fights, with Frith usually coming off better in the exchange. When she was 15 years old her parents tried to marry her off so she ran away from home. In an attempt to at least partially acknowledge their daughter's contrary and manly disposition, Frith was apprenticed to a saddler. She didn't take to it and the appointment was a failure.

As a last resort, at the suggestion of her uncle, Frith was sent overseas to America to work on the plantations. She was put on a merchant ship, but the vessel had barely left Gravesend when Mary Frith jumped into the Thames and swam back to shore. It was a weird form of inverted baptism that washed away all vestiges of a respectable life. From the time she re-entered London, she would be a professional criminal until the day she died.

Mary Frith became a pickpocket and was part of a gang that worked the Southwark Bear Gardens. She took to wearing men's clothes during this period. She suffered arrests and was locked up in many of London's numerous prisons; she was apparently branded four times for her crimes. She distanced

Mary Frith escaped from forced exile to America when she dived into the Thames and swam ashore at Gravesend. (Mark Nightingale)

herself from her gang when she was betrayed by one of her own. From that point on she sought to work out her criminal calling as an independent. In her varied career she was thought to have been (or else was accused of being) everything from a forger to a fortune teller to a whore.

Whatever the truth of the above, by the second decade of the seventeenth century Moll Cutpurse was an established figure in the rougher quarters of London society, and an ominous presence in the capital's taverns, tobacco shops and theatres. Most people knew who she was, but she polarised the city's population. It was impossible to have a neutral opinion of her. Her repudiation of the female dress code, her mannish habits and the rejection of the expected role of her gender caused offence as well as a great deal of conjecture about her sexuality. She was thought at times to be either a hermaphrodite or else bisexual. To many she was a folk hero. Her fame was such that she warranted the unprecedented distinction of being fictionalised on the London stage in her own lifetime. The play was *The Roaring Girl*.

THOMAS MIDDLETON

Middleton was the great theatrical advocate of contemporary seventeenth-century London life. He was born four years before Mary Frith in London

Thomas Middleton.

(possibly Limehouse) in 1580. His father was a bricklayer and reasonably wealthy but died when his son was only 5 years old. His mother remarried, but her choice of husband was disastrous; his name was Thomas Harvey and his motives for marriage were highly mercenary having lost a fortune investing in Walter Raleigh and Richard Grenville's doomed Roanoke expedition. The marriage was not a success and the next decade and a half were mired in legal squabbles as Harvey tried to seize control of the Middleton's modest fortune.

Thomas Middleton spent two years at Oxford University but didn't finish his degree. Instead he dabbled in poetry. The results were not considered particularly successful but there seemed to be a spark of promise. By 1601 Middleton had returned to London where he married. His brother-in-law was an actor for the prestigious Admiral's Men. This was probably Middleton's doorway into a career in theatre. By 1603 he was fully ensconced in the company's pool of talented writers.

The Admiral's Men was one of the foremost theatrical companies of the era. Presided over by the Tudor impresario Phillip Henslowe, the Admiral's Men operated in Southwark out of the Rose Theatre. The Rose was situated opposite the imposing structure of the Globe Theatre, home of the Lord Chamberlain's Men, the company for which Shakespeare wrote and was a shareholder. The two companies enjoyed a healthy rivalry and were amongst the great entrepreneurial successes of the Tudor and Jacobean age.

Tudor and Jacobean theatre was, paradoxically, the principal mass entertainment of the era that consistently managed to produce many of the most sophisticated and complex works in the English language. Theatre was also the great democratic institution as virtually all classes came together to watch a play, albeit kept physically separated by the pricing structure that allowed a person to stand for a penny or sit in the galleries on cushioned seats for three times that amount. The theatres tended to stage a different play each day, performed in the mid-afternoon in the open air. There was a rolling repertoire of popular plays but new material was in constant demand and so a sweatshop of talented and industrious writers was essential for the survival of any theatre company.

For a writer starting out in Tudor London, the normal trajectory was to serve as an apprentice to a more experienced writer and work in collaboration. In fact, collaborative work was the norm throughout much of a writer's career, however successfully or well regarded they became in their own right. Middleton learned quickly and seemed to improve with each engagement, writing on his own within a very quick space of time. The year 1602 was a year of apprenticeship. By 1603 Queen Elizabeth was dead and James I was on the throne of England. This was also the year that the plague emptied London. The theatres were closed and writers had to find other ways of making money. Middleton turned to pamphlet writing.

By 1604 the theatres were open again and Middleton's work was being performed before the new king. The period between 1604 and the beginning of the next decade saw Middleton embark on his first run of great plays. He began to specialise in a genre he was to subsequently dominate – the City Comedy, of which *The Roaring Girl* was one of his last examples. *A Chaste Maid at Cheapside*, *A Trick To Catch the Old One* and *A Mad World My Masters* are all skilful examples of Middleton's work in the genre that are still performed or in print today. The stories in Middleton's City Comedies were essentially sex comedies, in which the marriage prospects of likeable young noblemen were invariably opposed by the lecherous or avaricious machinations of their older relatives, before order was restored in the final act. Middleton was by turns filthy and witty. He had a great facility for writing female characters and his heroines were drawn with strength, dimension and empathy.

But the City Comedy's most charismatic character was London itself. The farcical story lines were played out within the geographical arena of a London recognisable to everyone in the audience. A sense of the vibrancy and chaos of city life is almost tangible in the text and must have been electric in its original performance. And where tragedy disdained to engage with contemporary law and order, Middleton's comedies had the frequent threat of London's debtors' prisons hanging over its protagonists' heads, with *The Roaring Girl* in particular providing an exhaustive view of the London criminal scene.[1]

THOMAS DEKKER

Much less is known about Dekker than Middleton. His years prior to his time as a playwright are a virtual blank. But what we do know of him is extremely dramatic and representative of how hazardous a writer's life could be in the Tudor and Jacobean times.

Dekker was born around 1572. His surname indicates that he may have been Dutch or else had Dutch lineage. Most historians and scholars assume a life spent in London; his work certainly expresses a detailed knowledge of and fascination with London life. What is certain is that by 1598 he was also one of Henslowe's writers for the Admiral's Men. His output was industrious. In 1598 alone he was known to have worked on sixteen plays. And he didn't just write for Henslowe. He was one of the era's great collaborators and his list of co-authors is formidable, including many of the best playwrights in the English language.[2] However, industry did not guarantee wealth. There was no royalty system in place, so playwrights (unless they became shareholders in theatrical companies) were dependent on a furious turnover of plays and other subsidiary writing to survive. Six pounds was considered an acceptable fee for a play. The fee would be broken down into two or three payments, beginning with an advance, concluding with a payment on delivery of the finished work, with a possible payment in between as scenes of the play were delivered to the company. It is apt to talk about money with regard to Dekker as he was

Thomas Dekker.

useless in managing it and was susceptible to debt. London's numerous debtors' prisons offered harsh conditions for those who could not meet their
financial obligations. In 1599 Dekker was imprisoned for debt and locked up
in the Poultry Counter; Phillip Henslowe secured his release.

By 1601 Dekker was embroiled in another controversy. The War of the
Poets was a literary feud started by the volatile playwright Ben Jonson. Jonson
was a spectacularly oversensitive, easily offended and vindictive man. By 1601
he already had a death on his conscience, having killed the actor Gabriel
Spencer in a duel. The playwright John Marston had included a portrait of
him in his work that Jonson took offence to (although it was doubtful that
offence was ever the intention). Jonson responded with an insulting version
of Marston in one of his works. Marston retaliated in kind, and the vendetta,
expressed in the flurry of plays written at incredible speed and performed
in the opposing structures of the Globe and the Rose, became one of the
commercial phenomena of the year. Dekker was dragged into the feud when
Jonson launched a completely gratuitous assault on him in his play *The
Poetaster*. Dekker's riposte was *Satiromatix* in which a barely disguised version
of Jonson was portrayed as vain and resentful. The feud eventually fizzled out
and cordial relations between authors (at least as far as Marston was concerned) were resumed.

Like Middleton, the plague of 1603 temporarily derailed Dekker's playwriting career, and, like Middleton, Dekker turned to writing pamphlets to
make his money. It was in this form that Thomas Dekker excelled, although
he would (perhaps unfairly) never be counted amongst the truly great writers
of the era. He had successes and his work was performed before King James,
but he produced too few enduring works that did not have shared author-
ship. As a pamphleteer he exhibited a dominance of the genre and provided a
window into much of what we know about Tudor and Jacobean London life.
When the theatres reopened and his playwriting career resumed, he would
continue to write pamphlets with great industry and skill.

Pamphlets were generally anonymous works. They were very popular
and their content could be anything from political or religious polemics to
reportage or moral satires. Dekker's work was essentially satirical. He chronicled the ravages of the plague in *The Wonderful Year* (1603); he attacked the
pretensions of the shallow and fashion obsessed (as well as providing a very
detailed account of a trip to the theatre) in *The Gulls Horn-Book* (1609); he
also described the various scams and schemes of London's underworld in *The
Bellmen of London* (1608) and *Lantern and Candlelight* (1609). The latter two
pamphlets are not believed to have been drawn from any great personal association with the underworld. Much of what Dekker wrote on this subject
owed a lot to existing works on the same topic. But his chapters describing

life in London's prisons bare the stamp of the bitter personal experience of having served time in the debtors' gaols of the capital.

Amongst Dekker's many collaborators was Thomas Middleton. When the theatres reopened in 1604 the two writers worked together on the commercially successful drama *The Honest Whore Part One*. They would come together half a decade later to write *The Roaring Girl*.

THE ROARING GIRL

The plot of *The Roaring Girl* is very simple. Young nobleman Sebastian Wengrave wishes to marry Mary Fitz-Allard. His father Sir Alexander Wengrave opposes the match on economic grounds. Sebastian retaliates by engaging the help of Moll, the Roaring Girl. He aims to force his father into consenting to the match by persuading him that his alternative choice of bride is the cross-dressing outlaw Moll. Sir Alexander employs the London cutthroat Trapdoor to aid him in his stratagems to discredit and destroy Moll. There are numerous subplots, but the spine of *The Roaring Girl's* narrative is a duel of wits as Moll frustrates the various snares laid by Sir Alexander and manoeuvres him towards giving his consent to his son's preferred choice of bride.

The Moll Cutpurse of *The Roaring Girl* is loud and aggressive. She smokes good quality tobacco, is a skilful player of the viol and wears men's clothes, specifically 'a shag ruff, a frieze jerkin, a short sword, and a saveguard'. She is a physical force of nature, constantly in motion, described as having 'the spirit of four great parishes'. She is happy to aid Sebastian and Mary but rejects the thought of marriage for herself. She is portrayed as androgynous to some. Trapdoor refers to her 'Masculine womanhood' and describes her as a 'stout girl'. To others she is highly sexualised. Laxton, the lecherous nobleman (and minor villain) of *The Roaring Girl*, sees Moll as the 'wench' with whom he 'would give too much money to be nibbling with'. He is later humiliated by Moll when he mistakes her for a whore, arranges what he thinks is a liaison and is subsequently wounded by her in a swordfight. Moll is the consummate independent, declaring 'I please myself and care not who else loves me'. Ultimately, *The Roaring's Girl's* Moll is a ferocious, wild, tarnished guardian angel. She operates outside the law and society's strict conventions but is essentially moral, persecuting the hypocritical, the sexually predatory and the corrupt with a mixture of guile and physical force.

The London of *The Roaring Girl* is conveyed with a great sense of the salacious bustle of Jacobean capital life. Moll's Holborn is described as 'such a wrangling street', full of 'such jostling, as if everyone we met were drunk and reeled'. An impression of the immense river traffic that rowed Londoners to and fro across the Thames is conveyed in a chase towards the end of the play,

Moll Cutpurse. (Illustrated by Stephen Dennis)

as Sir Alexander tries to intercept his son and Moll when he is tricked into believing that they have run away to Lambeth to marry.

The Roaring Girl wears its knowledge of the practices and geography of the London underworld on its sleeve. Sir Alexander's henchman Trapdoor has been branded. Trapdoor and Moll conduct a conversation entirely in cant, the invented language of Tudor and Jacobean thieves. London's Chick Lane is described as a haunt of thieves. The Fortune Theatre (where *The Roaring Girl* would be performed) is mentioned in the context of an alleged assault by two butchers on a gentleman (a crime that may have actually happened). Trapdoor and his lackey, Tearcat, practise a con in which they masquerade as disabled war veterans in order to beg for money. But special attention is devoted to (and contempt poured all over) London's debtors' prisons. Poultry Counter, the prison where Dekker himself was locked up, is described as 'a park in which all the wild beasts of the city run head to head'. Sergeant Curtilax and his Yeoman, whose job is to catch debtors and drag them to the Counter, are described as 'carrion' and 'ravens'. When Moll fights Sergeant Curtilax and rescues a debtor from his clutches, it is hard not to interpret this as a wish-fulfilment revenge fantasy of Thomas Dekker.

Dekker's influence is all over the underworld sequences of *The Roaring Girl*. Middleton's incredible facility with dramatising strong, three-dimensional women is evident, as is his contempt for the highborn men who prey on them. Middleton and Dekker can claim equal credit for creating a vivid, living, breathing London. As far as their depiction of a real-life criminal eccentric goes, *The Roaring Girl* could almost have been written with Mary Frith looking over both writers' shoulders, making suggestions and giving her assent. The Jacobean outlaw is presented in a fashion that could not have failed to please her. She was known to have had a great love of the theatre and there is strong evidence to suggest that she was present at a performance of *The Roaring Girl* and got into trouble as a consequence.

FRITH AT THE FORTUNE

Mary Frith had two documented brushes with the law around the time of the performance of *The Roaring Girl*. In 1612 she was forced to do penance at St Paul's Cross. The event was witnessed by a John Chamberlain who wrote an account of what he saw in a letter to his patron Dudley Carlton. Chamberlain, who clearly disapproved of Frith, described her as 'a notorious baggage that used to go in man's apparel'. Frith responded to the punishment in a way unbecoming of Middleton and Dekker's version of her. She 'wept bitterly, and seemed very penitent', although Chamberlain conceded that she was 'maudlin drunk' on 'three quarts of sack'. In spite of her obvious humiliation, Frith did manage to claw back something of a moral victory. When the preacher began his address, Mary Frith responded by preaching her own sermon, relaying her own misdeeds and avowals to mend her ways to an increasingly growing crowd. Unfortunately for the preacher, who according to Chamberlain 'did

The commemorative plaque marking the location of the Fortune Theatre. (Mark Nightingale)

extremely badly', he was forced to watch his congregation migrate to Mary Frith, the more charismatic and gifted orator.

Frith's other clash with the law was an incident centred around an appearance at the Fortune Theatre. Henslowe and his business partner Edward Alleyn, a former actor who had been the first to perform many of Christopher Marlowe's great tragic heroes, had built the playhouse in 1600. Situated north of the Thames, the Fortune was designed as the new home for the Admiral's Men, a pragmatic response to the fact that they were losing commercial ground to the Globe. The Fortune's location attempted to exploit the pool of wealthy suburbanites who otherwise would have had to travel across the river to see a quality performance of a decent play. But the audiences that turned up were the usual mix of high and low, rough and gentile, the perfect audience for *The Roaring Girl* which received its premier on the Fortune's stage.

The play contains an epilogue that would have tantalised the original audience with the possibility of an appearance by the real Roaring Girl:

> Both crave your pardons: if what both have done
> Cannot full pay your expectation,
> The Roaring Girl herself, some few days hence,
> Shall on this stage give larger recompense.

Mary Frith did indeed crash the stage at the Fortune around this time and was hauled over the coals for it. The *Consistory of London Correction Book's* entry for 27 January 1611 chronicles Frith's appearance before the authorities to give an account of numerous complaints that had been made against her. Among the usual litany of objections about her male attire, whoredom, pimping, the criminal company she kept, her love of alehouses, foul language and blasphemy, was the accusation that she appeared on stage during a performance at the Fortune Theatre, playing the lute and singing a song, dressed as a man.

In the complaint against her, Mary Frith's association with the theatre is given a lot of weight. She is observed to have attended the theatre 'three quarts of the year'. This was not illegal but considered morally questionable by many of the Puritan authorities; but as royalty and the gentry clearly loved the plays there was little to be done but disapprove. Yet women performing on stage were a different matter. This was illegal (women's roles being played by boys). So Mary Frith's impromptu addition to the afternoon's entertainment was against the law.

It is not known what play Mary Frith attended when she committed her crime, but the circumstantial evidence seems to point towards *The Roaring Girl*. The dates roughly add up. The promise of a personal appearance in the play's text had been made and Mary Frith clearly loved an audience. The fact that she played the lute and sang a song correlates directly with a scene in the play where Moll Cutpurse does exactly that. If this were true, the audience would hardly have forgotten the moment when a tall woman, dressed and armed like a man, stepped onto the Fortune's stage and played herself for a scene or so.

THE REAL LIFE AND DEATH OF MRS MARY FRITH

The Roaring Girl wasn't the only work to reference the outlaw in her lifetime, nor was it the first to have done so. John Day had written a book about her in 1610. In 1611 Thomas Dekker made another reference to her in *If this be not a good play, the Devil is in it*. In 1614 Nathaniel Lovall's play, *Amends for Ladies*, included a much less complimentary version of Mary Frith in which she receives a dressing down for her androgyny. Even as late as 1632, Frith's skills as a receiver of stolen goods were being referenced in the play *The Court Beggar*.

The most exhaustive work on Frith was published in 1662, three years after her death. In *The Real Life and Death of Mrs Mary Frith Commonly Called Moll Cutpurse* the thief narrates her own life. It is a digressive narrative that contains reasonably detailed information about the workings of the Tudor and Jacobean criminal scene. The version of Moll that emerges is an ostentatious criminal and influential thief, surrounding herself with exotic pets like bulldogs, parrots, apes and squirrels, and keeping company with colourful criminal associates like Mul-Sack the Chimney Sweep and Corrington the Cheat. Her penance at St Paul's is mentioned. She travels across London on horseback, dressed in male clothing, blowing a trumpet and carrying a banner, until a mob takes offence and chases her. She has a vengeful streak, meting out creative retribution on a constable that had previously arrested her and a servant that has the temerity to call her 'Mal Cutpurse', a nickname she hates. The work goes to great pains to distance Moll from any charge of being a hermaphrodite. A real hermaphrodite named Aniseed-Water Robin makes an appearance for the narrative purpose of being humiliated by Moll, who does not approve of his condition.

The Real Life and Death of Mrs Mary Frith follows Moll's story into the middle years of the seventeenth century, long after the deaths of Middleton and Dekker. In fact, Mary Frith outlived the two playwrights by quite a margin. Once Middleton and Dekker had parted company with their criminal muse, Mary Frith's greatest advocates' lives and careers took divergent paths.

AFTER *THE ROARING GIRL*

Any trouble Thomas Dekker had been in prior to the writing of *The Roaring Girl* was eclipsed by the events that were to follow. In 1613 he was once again arrested for debt and served a mammoth seven years in the King's Bench Prison. The sentence effectively destroyed the momentum of his writing career. His professional life, post-release, included some collaborative work for the theatre, but even then controversy stayed with him. Apart from *The Roaring Girl*, Dekker's other foray into Jacobean true crime was a play called *Keep the Widow Waking*, written in collaboration with John Ford, John Webster and William Rowley. It drew on two separate but very recent London-based incidents: the murder of a mother by her son; and the kidnapping and attempted forced marriage of Anne Eldson (a 62-year-old widow) by Tobias Audley and his gang. The motive for the forced marriage was financial.

The play was performed in the less fashionable surroundings of the Red Bull Theatre in Clerkenwell, while Audley's trial was still in progress. It was alleged during the trial that Audley himself had encouraged the play to be written in order to humiliate Eldson. A libel writ was issued. Dekker had to give evidence but appeared to walk away from the debacle without censure. But it was all too much for Anne Eldson, who died before the trial had concluded.

Thomas Dekker died in 1632, in all probability still owing money. His widow 'renounced administration of his estate', a legal technique employed to avoid incurring someone else's debt.

Thomas Middleton fared much better, with one crippling exception. His writing career went from strength to strength. Having mastered the City Comedy, in the latter stages of his career he became the great Jacobean tragedian. He wrote *The Changeling* and *Women Beware Women*, and he is strongly believed to have collaborated with Shakespeare on *Macbeth*. *The Revenger's Tragedy* (for a long time attributed to Cyril Tourneur) is now by common academic assent listed as a Middleton play. His long, successful and versatile career as a playwright was brought to an ignominious end with his greatest commercial success. In 1624 Middleton's *A Game at Chess* almost caused an international incident. Performed by the King's Men at the Globe Theatre, the play was a transparent attack on Spain. The Spanish ambassador, Don Carlos Coloma, was held up to a very personal form of ridicule. The actor playing the ambassador's theatrical surrogate actually wore some of the diplomat's old clothes and much was made of an anal medical complaint that the ambassador was known to suffer from. The play ran for an unprecedented nine consecutive performances and the smallest audience it boasted was 3,000. It would have run for longer but was shut down, the company was hauled before the Privy Council and bound over for £300. They were then banned from

The reconstruction of the Globe Theatre. (Mark Nightingale)

performing until the king decided otherwise. Middleton was ordered to appear but failed to answer his summons. He went to ground and his son appeared in his stead. Middleton surfaced a few days later and may have served time in prison. It was the end of his playwriting career, but he received the consolatory prize of being made the official chronicler of the City of London, a post he held until his death in 1627.

FRITH & FAIRFAX

Neither Middleton nor Dekker lived to see it, but as dramatists they would have salivated over the greatest criminal exploit ever attributed to Mary Frith. Unfortunately, by the time it was deemed to have happened there were no theatres to stage her adventures, and neither playwright would have anticipated or recognised the political and social landscape of England in Moll Cutpurse's final years.

Mary Frith endured the Civil War and lived through much of the Protectorate. She was a zealous Royalist, and hated Cromwell, his generals and administrators. She carried on her criminal activities throughout these years but her work was now framed in a political context. Her criminal

Sir Thomas Fairfax, the Earl of Essex.

enterprises were subsequently interpreted less as the anti-social acts of a
popular but essentially self-serving thief, and more as the subversive deeds
of an unreconstructed rebel holding the fort, like Robin Hood, until God's
ordained monarch replaced a vile usurper.

The Real Life and Death of Mrs Mary Frith dramatises Moll's Civil War years.
In it she claims: 'I think I was the only declared person in our street against

Parliament.' She describes Parliament as 'those modern thieves'. She and her gang best a bunch of Roundheads in a physical confrontation. She insults Parliamentarian soldiers and is struck by a stick for her impertinence. She refuses to join the women who help prepare London's siege defences. In an atypically diplomatic moment she is part of an all-female delegation that petitions Parliament for peace, but who are effectively told to go home and do the dishes. She reserves her harshest contempt for Cromwell's great general, Sir Thomas Fairfax, who lived near her. Frith dresses her bulldog in Essex colours and describes Fairfax as 'no woman's man and therefore very obnoxious to me'.

The most celebrated act ever attributed to Mary Frith was performed against Thomas Fairfax. The Roundhead general and two of his servants were crossing Hounslow Heath in daylight when they were confronted by a mounted and armed Mary Frith. She robbed the general at gunpoint before shooting him in the arm. She took 250 gold Jacobuses from him, killed his servants' horses and left the general bleeding on the Heath. A chase followed as Roundhead soldiers stationed nearby pursued Mary Frith on horseback as far as Turnham Green. Frith's horse went lame, and the soldiers caught up with her and arrested her. She was imprisoned at Newgate and ought to have been hanged. But, impressed by the incredible panache she had shown in the execution of her crime, Fairfax was believed to have interceded on her behalf. She was given the option of buying her freedom at the exorbitantly high price of £2,000. She could afford it. She paid up and was set free.

In the tangled mythology of Frith's life, the Fairfax incident is so ubiquitous that it is often relayed as fact; in actuality, the only account of it was

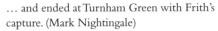

The mythic chase between Moll Frith and her roundhead pursuers began at Hounslow Heath …

… and ended at Turnham Green with Frith's capture. (Mark Nightingale)

written in the eighteenth century by the plagiaristic and unreliable writer Captain Alexander Smith. *The Real Life and Death of Mrs Mary Frith* doesn't mention the incident at all. In all probability the assault on Fairfax is a potent and entertaining fiction.

Frith died in 1659 of dropsy; she was in her mid-70s. Buried at St Brides Church in her beloved Fleet Street, there was thought to be little left of the large fortune she had accrued over her long criminal career. Her will was said to have bequeathed £20 to her friends to drink the health of King Charles II when he was restored to the throne.

St Brides Church: Mary Frith's burial place. (Mark Nightingale)

4

TWO 'SPECTABLE OLD GENTLEMEN

BOZ

Oliver Twist was only Charles Dickens' second novel. Its publication would establish him as a commercial and critical phenomenon, a position he would maintain until he died. His route to success had been extremely difficult, yet it had qualified him beyond his peers to write the definitive novel of nineteenth-century suffering in the over-arching context of the Victorian underworld.

Dickens' childhood was happy. The best part of it was spent in Chatham, where he enjoyed a good education and access to a host of stimulating and exotic reading material. His father, John Dickens, worked for the naval pay office as a clerk, and his job took him to London. But John Dickens was bad with money. His financial incompetence led to his arrest for debt and he was confined in Marshalsea Gaol. Dickens' education was derailed and he was forced to suffer the double indignity of getting a job in a blacking factory and eating his morning and evening meals at the debtors' prison. Dickens was 12 years old at the time. The work was hard and the conditions were difficult. One of Dickens' compatriots was a young man named Bob Fagin.

Dickens' education resumed when his father was released from prison. In 1827 he got a job as an office boy at a law firm. His aptitude for shorthand led to work as a court reporter. By the early 1830s he had graduated to covering debates in the House of Lords. He worked for a handful of periodicals such as *The True Son, The Mirror of Parliament* and *The Morning Chronicle*. Under the pseudonym Boz, Dickens specialised in writing sketches. Sketches were satiric or journalistic pieces that shed light on any aspect of contemporary life that took Dickens' interest. One of the constants was his obsession with the hidden and often seamy side of London life. The best remembered of

Charles Dickens.

Fagin. (Illustrated by
Jean Nightingale)

Dickens' sketches was about a trip he made to Newgate Gaol, the great old anachronistic dungeon that had caged Jack Sheppard and Jonathan Wild, and would provide the stage for the vicious epilogue of *Oliver Twist*.

By this stage Dickens could afford to live in a nice house in a decent area, but he was literally streets away from Field Lane and Saffron Hill, violent and squalid areas avoided by people of means. Compared to his contemporaries, Dickens took an atypical interest in these locations. He made a point of visiting them. They would become the playground of *Oliver Twist*'s villain Fagin.

MUDFOG

Dickens' journalism was collated in the publication *Sketches by Boz*. He retained the pseudonym Boz for his first work of fiction – a comic novel entitled *The Posthumous Adventures of the Pickwick Club*. Dickens began writing *Oliver Twist* while *Pickwick* was still being serialised. It would be the first book to which he would ascribe his actual name.

The literary genesis of *Oliver Twist* was indirect. In 1837 Dickens wrote a short piece called *The Public Life of Mr Tulrumble* for the new magazine *Bentley's Miscellany*. Based on the Chatham of his youth, Dickens set his story in a fictitious town he named Mudfog. He then wrote a second Mudfog story, in which the subject was a baby born in the workhouse. The story mutated into the opening sections of *Oliver Twist*, which began to appear in serialised form in February 1837. Dickens siphoned much of his childhood misery into the narrative. The journalist and the polemicist in Dickens would also get their airing as he applied his knowledge of London's underbelly and raged against the injustices of the country's Poor Laws. During the writing of the novel, Dickens suffered bereavement. The death of his sister-in-law, upon whom he doted, undoubtedly cast a further shadow over the narrative. All these elements flavoured what began as a satirical work, but turned into something altogether more intense. And out of this confluence of influences emerged a villain that would get under Dickens' skin in ways even he did not fully understand. He would admit that he felt almost haunted by Fagin as he was writing *Oliver Twist*. He would confide to his friend James Fields that Fagin was 'such an out and outer I don't know what to do with him'.

A MURDEROUS MELODRAMA

The plot of *Oliver Twist* is complicated. The young hero of the title is born in the workhouse of a nameless estuary town. His disgraced mother dies in childbirth and he is raised by the inmates of the workhouse who mistreat him. He is apprenticed to a coffin maker. He escapes and arrives half-starved in London, where he is adopted by a gang of child thieves and introduced to their leader, Fagin, and his associates, the brutal thief Bill Sikes and his mistress Nancy. Yet Oliver is not really the penniless orphan he appears to be. There is a contested inheritance, an incriminating locket and an evil half-brother named Monks. Fagin and Monks turn out to be partners in crime. Lacking the resolve to simply kill Oliver, Monks employs Fagin to mind the boy and so steep him in the criminal lifestyle as to render him indictable, the law ultimately doing what Monks hasn't got the guts to do himself. Oliver is falsely arrested, rescued and placed into the custody of Brownlow, a kindly gentleman. Oliver is kidnapped, taken on a burglary by Sikes, shot, left for dead in the countryside and nursed back to health by Rose (a young woman who happens to be the half-sister of his dead mother). Nancy has an attack of conscience. She exposes Monks and authenticates Oliver's true identity. For her perceived treachery she is murdered by Sikes. The hue and cry that follows destroys Fagin and his organisation.

Dickens, in the early passages of *Oliver Twist*, composes the narrative in the broader context of 'all good murderous melodramas'. But the ostensible plot of *Oliver Twist* is secondary in most readers' memories to the more immediate attraction of Oliver's adventures in the heart of criminal London. The power of these passages as standalone sequences is testified to by the number of subsequent theatre, film and television adaptations that have jettisoned everything to do with Monks, Rose and Oliver's noble birth, streamlining the drama to its dramatic essentials: the workhouse prologue, London, Fagin, Sikes, Dodger, Nancy, and by extension Brownlow.

FAGIN

Oliver hears about Fagin before he ever sees him. John Dawkins, aka the Artful Dodger, the dandified teenage pickpocket who befriends Oliver and guides him through London, describes his benefactor Fagin as 'a 'spectable old gentleman'. Oliver is taken to meet Fagin at his den near Field Lane. Fagin is surrounded by children smoking tobacco who buzz around their master like scruffy courtiers. Dickens describes Fagin like this:

> In a frying-pan, which was on the fire, and which was secured to the mantelshelf by a string, some sausages were cooking; and standing over them, with a toasting-fork in his hand, was a very old shrivelled Jew, whose villainous-looking and repulsive face was obscured by a quantity of matted

red hair. He was dressed in a greasy flannel gown, with his throat bare; and seemed to be dividing his attention between the frying-pan and the clothes-horse, over which a great number of silk handkerchiefs were hanging.

The description is an unsettling mix of the demonic and the domestic. Fagin talks to himself a lot. He rubs his hands a great deal. He has black nails and most of his teeth are gone. He is furtive, deceptively agile and constantly alert. His senses are sharper than anybody else in the novel. When he is angry his voice is described as 'something between a mad bull and a speaking trumpet'. He is often seen in the context of food and drink, either cooking sausages, toasting bread or making coffee. He is referred to constantly as the 'merry old gentleman'. For most of his initial encounters with Oliver, Fagin is paternal and playful. Of course, he is slowly inducting Oliver into a life of thievery. Oliver is unaware of what is happening, but Fagin does it gently, famously teaching Oliver to pick pockets by way of a game wherein he trails handkerchiefs out of his own coat, encouraging Oliver to take them without him noticing. Fagin is described as a 'fence', a receiver of stolen goods. But Fagin also has his army of child thieves and adult criminal associates with whom he works closely. The most notable of these is Bill Sikes and Bill's lover Nancy – a violent professional burglar and a young woman who is in all probability a prostitute.[1]

Fagin is traditionally remembered by those who have either never read the book or whose memories are coloured by its numerous adaptations as a sort of dysfunctional father figure to Oliver. What Fagin is doing is clearly wrong (he is occasionally heavy-handed with Oliver, and the very nature of his profession might result in Oliver's imprisonment or worse), but relative to the treatment that has already been meted out to Oliver in the workhouse, Fagin treats him well. The blame for the physical danger Oliver later finds himself in is traditionally laid at the feet of Bill Sikes and Fagin's inability to control his violent business partner. However, Fagin, as Dickens wrote him, is by far the most dangerous, manipulative and quietly vicious character in the novel. The first glimpse of this is when Oliver wakes up in Fagin's den and observes the old thief examining the best of his stolen jewellery. Fagin has taken the jewellery from a secret hiding place. He doesn't initially notice Oliver, but when he does, he worries that Oliver has seen the hiding place. He picks up a knife and interrogates the boy, at one point seeming to contemplate whether it would be prudent to cut him. Later in the novel, after Oliver has escaped Fagin's influence, been recaptured and re-inducted, Fagin's methods of controlling him are a mixture of the conciliatory and the extremely violent, at one point threatening him with a club.

THE ROUGH MAN & THE WITHERED OLD FENCE

The true nature of Fagin is never more revealing than when he is dealing with Bill Sikes, and by extension Sikes' lover Nancy. Dickens describes Sikes as:

> a stoutly-built fellow of about five-and-thirty, in a black velveteen coat, very soiled drab breeches, lace-up half boots, and grey cotton stockings which inclosed a bulky pair of legs, with large swelling calves; – the kind of legs, which in such costume, always look in an unfinished and incomplete state without a set of fetters to garnish them … a broad heavy countenance with a beard of three days' growth, and two scowling eyes; one of which displayed various parti-coloured symptoms of having been recently damaged by a blow.

Fagin describes Sikes as 'a rough man' who 'thinks nothing of blood when his own is up'. Sikes describes Fagin as respectively a 'withered old fence', a 'black hearted wolf' and 'the old 'un', a euphemism for Satan himself. On the surface their relationship is an uneasy business alliance, with Fagin expending a large amount of his energy negotiating Sikes' dangerous moods, often placating Sikes by conceding more money to the burglar than is his due. Sikes and Fagin seem to put up with each other out of necessity. Fagin provides the criminal administration Sikes is not capable of. Sikes is a highly skilled burglar and a valuable source of revenue. His violent nature, although two-edged, would also seem to provide a degree of protection to Fagin and his gang. On paper Sikes would appear to be the more dangerous of the two men, but Sikes is ultimately less deadly because he is predictable. Fagin has a temper that even Sikes momentarily recoils from when the fence's blood is hot. But it is Fagin's genius for manipulation and the accumulation of criminal intelligence that marks him as the more lethal of the two men. At numerous times in *Oliver Twist*, Fagin reminds his associates that he has access to information that could hang any one of them should he see fit. Fagin tells Oliver a cautionary tale about an ungrateful boy thief he had once had framed and executed. Later on, Fagin describes himself as 'I, that knows so much, and could hang so many besides myself!' But Fagin's greatest weapon is his ability to play people off against each other. It is a skill he exercises at the novel's climax, and a skill that exposes him as a creature whose core nature is utterly predatory.

THE DEATH OF NANCY

When Nancy is going behind both Sikes' and Fagin's back to clear Oliver's name, Fagin is quick to deduce that she is up to something. He jumps to the wrong conclusion, surmising that Nancy has a new lover. Fagin knows that Sikes would kill Nancy if she left him for another man. It is revealed at this point that Fagin hates Sikes and wants rid of him. The main motive seems to be a mixture of pragmatism and hurt feelings: 'Sikes knew too much, and his ruffian taunts had not galled Fagin the less, because the wounds were hidden.' Fagin determines to have Nancy followed. Once he has accumulated enough incriminating information, he plans to blackmail Nancy into murdering Sikes by having her poison him. When the true nature of Nancy's disloyalty becomes apparent to Fagin, he is furious. Sikes, who moments previously had been a liability to Fagin, is now a weapon to be wielded by the old thief. Fagin approaches Sikes and traps him into taking action against Nancy with a series of hypothetical questions. In an intense sequence that reads like a satanic inversion of the Biblical account of Abraham pleading with God for the lives of the righteous, Fagin asks Sikes what he would do if various members of their gang informed on him. Sikes' response is always the same: he would kill them. Fagin leaves Nancy until last, then finally reveals that she has turned on them whereupon Sikes leaves in a murderous fury. Fagin cautions him:

> 'Hear me speak a word,' rejoined Fagin, laying his hand upon the lock. 'You won't be –'
> 'Well,' replied the other.
> 'You won't be – too – violent, Bill?'
> The day was breaking, and there was light enough for the men to see each other's faces. They exchanged one brief glance; there was a fire in the eyes of both, which could not be mistaken.
> 'I mean,' said Fagin, showing that he felt all disguise was now useless, 'not too violent for safety. Be crafty, Bill, and not too bold.'

Fagin's intention is clear. He is as complicit in the murder of Nancy as Sikes is. He wants Sikes to kill Nancy, but he also wants Sikes to be discreet about the murder he is about to commit. Sikes is anything but discreet, and in one of English literature's most upsetting sequences he uses the butt of a pistol and then a club to beat Nancy to death. He leaves the body unburied and goes on the run, dogged by what he believes is Nancy's spirit watching him just out of eyesight. Sikes has his last stand in the dockland slum of Jacobs Island. He dies on a rooftop trying to swing down to the muddy bank. The rope slips and he hangs himself.

DOWNFALL

The fallout from Nancy's murder puts pay to most of Fagin's gang. Noah Claypole, the minion sent by Fagin to spy on Nancy, informs on Fagin. Fagin's arrest takes place off the page but it is reported that he narrowly avoids being lynched by an angry mob. The novel rejoins Fagin at his trial during the judge's summing up. The crowd is hostile but the chapter assumes something of Fagin's perspective as he silently observes all and sundry who catch his attention. He is distracted but paradoxically he is also observant and fully aware of what is about to befall him. Fagin is found guilty and he receives the death sentence. When asked by the judge why he shouldn't be hanged, Fagin half-heartedly answers that he is 'an old man'.

Fagin is taken to the condemned cell in Newgate Gaol. He is verbally abused en route. His mind begins to fragment as he thinks about hanged men he has known. He feels that his cell is full of executed compatriots and calls for a light. He rages, blasphemes and refuses spiritual comfort. His behaviour unnerves the guards. By the time Oliver and Brownlow visit Fagin his mind has gone. Brownlow wants access to papers Monks has left in Fagin's possession. Fagin is in no position to help them. In his madness he tries to enlist Oliver to help him escape and grabs the boy. Dickens describes the last time we see Fagin:

> The men laid hands upon him, and disengaging Oliver from his grasp, held him back. He struggled with the power of desperation, for an instant; and then sent up cry upon cry that penetrated even those massive walls, and rang in their ears until they reached the open yard.

Fagin's hanging happens off the page and is not described.

Once Fagin has been disposed of there is only one chapter left in the novel and it is barely a chapter at all. Entitled 'And last', the final chapter in *Oliver Twist* is a summing-up of the numerous fates, happy and sad, that await all the surviving characters. But the real climax of the story is Fagin's downfall. It is a testament to the way Fagin had crawled under Dickens' skin and wrested the focus of attention away from the title character of the novel and onto its principal villain.

'THE JEW'

Fagin is a problematic character. He is, in part, an anti-Semitic creation. For large chunks of *Oliver Twist* Fagin is described simply as 'the Jew'. Despite Dickens' often unconvincing protests to the contrary, Fagin's ethnicity is undoubtedly linked to his criminality. In later editions of *Oliver Twist*, Dickens appears to make partial amends when, in the latter sections of the novel, he alters the amount of times he refers to Fagin as 'the Jew'. The character of Rhia, a kindly Jew in Dickens' later novel *Our Mutual Friend*, has been interpreted as a form of reparation for the offence caused by Fagin. But whatever the true nature of Dickens' actual, or perceived, anti-Semitism, he was not alone in the literary world, nor was he the worst offender. Around about the same time *Oliver Twist* was being read by an eager public, Dickens' contemporary, William Harrison Ainsworth, had scored a huge success with his novel about Jack Sheppard, which contained a truly repellent two-dimensional Jewish villain. Dickens was a far better writer than Ainsworth, and whatever the true depth of his antipathy towards Jews might have been, Fagin was undoubtedly created with a previously unprecedented degree of skill, precision and even love. In fact, all the villains in the novel dominate the narrative whenever they are on the page. They are missed when they are not around. Often, *Oliver Twist* flags as a consequence of their absence. However vile and objectionable the novel's villains are, they have more dimensions than the majority of its heroes, who are more often than not paper-thin caricatures of virtue. The villains, by contrast, are never less than human, each exhibiting traits that make them at the very least pitiable creations: Monks' fear of thunder, the terror and the shreds of remorse in the fugitive Sikes, and Nancy's heartbreaking sense of her own predetermined doom. Fagin is not exempt. His eventual degradation elicits pity in the reader in spite of every vile thing he is responsible for. In many respects, Fagin is the most human character in *Oliver Twist*.

LONDON

Of all the writers featured in this book, Dickens' love affair with London is the most vivid. Whereas most of the writers profiled within these pages take a slightly more impressionistic approach to describing aspects of the capital city, Dickens loses himself in the details of the metropolis. *Oliver Twist* is an embarrassment of riches in terms of getting a sense of the odours, sights and textures of 1830s London. Many of the novel's characters spend much of their time walking across huge tracts of the city: Oliver is led into London by the Artful Dodger; Oliver is kidnapped by Nancy and Sikes and dragged away from the sanctuary of Mr Brownlow's home through fog-shrouded Spitalfields; Bill Sikes takes Oliver on an epic forced march en route to a burglary, beginning in Whitechapel and passing through Spitalfields and Bethnal Green. There is a hiatus where Sikes and Fagin talk business, and then the trek resumes taking in Finsbury Square, Barbican, Long Lane, Holborn, Hyde Park, Kensington,

Chiswick, Kew, Brentford and eventually Hampton. In that one journey London is described in the dead of night and as it is waking up. Each of the above descriptions is choice. All of them are quotable. But one passage will have to stand for the whole: in the messy aftermath of Sikes' burglary, when news reaches Fagin that Oliver has been shot, the old thief careers through Snow Hill, Holborn Hill and Saffron Hill trying to gather information about the disaster. Dickens describes the Thieves' Market in Field Lane that Fagin passes through:

> Confined as the limits of Field Lane are, it has its barber, its coffee-shop, its beer-shop, and its fried-fish warehouse. It is a commercial colony of itself: the emporium of petty larceny: visited at early morning, and setting-in of dusk, by silent merchants, who traffic in dark back-parlours, and who go as strangely as they come. Here, the clothesman, the shoe-vamper, and the rag-merchant, display their goods, as sign-boards to the petty thief; here, stores of old iron and bones, and heaps of mildewy fragments of woollen-stuff and linen, rust and rot in the grimy cellars.

Dickens had visited most of the areas he wrote about. He had been to Newgate. He would attend at least two highly publicised executions.[2] He would cultivate a friendship with the revered Scotland Yard detective Charles Field,[3] who would personally guide him through some of the very worst slums in London. The journalistic integrity of Dickens' rendering of the London underworld is extremely accurate. Criminal practices common at the time become many of the incidental details that flavour *Oliver Twist*. One of Oliver's first tasks under Fagin's tutelage is to pick away any distinguishing markings on handkerchiefs that might betray them as stolen property. An offhand mention is made of the treadmill at the House of Correction, a feared and debilitating form of hard labour. Fagin talks in cant when recruiting Noah Claypole. He makes reference to the 'kinchin lay', an actual form of theft in which young boys running errands were tripped up and their money taken from them. Fagin's practice of enlisting children to do his stealing was a known form of criminal enterprise. It had its own name. As well as being a fence, in the parlance of the underworld Fagin was also a 'kidsman'.

Few of the reading public at the time appeared to be neutral about having this world presented to them in the form of a novel. Most of them loved the book. *Oliver Twist* was incredibly popular – but there were the inevitable bones of contention. The poet Richard Hengist Horne felt that too much empathy was shown towards its criminal characters. The violence was criticised, leading to an embargo on stage adaptations by the Lord Chamberlain.[4] The most absurd criticism came from Sir Peter Laurie, an alderman who took issue with

Dickens' description of Jacobs Island, the dockland setting of Bill Sikes' death. Laurie claimed that no such place existed, that Dickens had made it up. It was an arrogant accusation, as Laurie could have simply gone there and had a look, had he the nerve to risk robbery or cholera. Laurie's appalling attitude was symptomatic of many moneyed Londoners who refused to acknowledge the appalling conditions that existed often yards away from where they lived. Dickens would be vindicated. Dickens did not need an advocate, but nevertheless, the extraordinary journalist Henry Mayhew corroborated much of what he wrote in his fiction. Mayhew's great life's work was the meticulous chronicling of the lives, professions and living conditions of London's honest poor and its criminal professionals. He even managed to settle the conundrum of whether Jacobs Island existed by taking the radical step of actually going there and seeing for himself.

Today, the integrity of Dickens' research is rarely questioned. His writing, be it fiction or non-fiction, is seen as an important and reliable window into the criminal terrain of the nineteenth century. We know now that the majority of what he wrote about in *Oliver Twist* was based on real criminal practice. But was Fagin based on a real criminal?

THOSE PETTICOAT LANERS

There was certainly a Jewish criminal subculture that operated in and around the areas described in *Oliver Twist*. Henry Mayhew interviewed a young pickpocket who had inside knowledge of how Jewish thieves performed their trade in London's East End. With great venom the anonymous pickpocket substantiates much of the criminal practice Dickens ascribes to Fagin, as well as providing a peephole into how Jews were regarded by many at the time.

> The Jews in Petticoat Lane are terrible rogues; They'll buy anything of you – they'll buy what you've stolen from their next-door neighbours – that they would if they knew it. But they'll give you very little for it, and they threaten to give you up if you won't take a quarter of the value of it. 'Oh! I shee you do it,' they say, 'and I like to shee him robbed, but you musht take vot I give.' I wouldn't mind what harm came to those Petticoat Laners. Many of them are worth thousands, though you wouldn't think it.

Still alive when *Oliver Twist* was being written, there was one Jewish thief who many believe lays the strongest claim to being the real-life inspiration for Dickens' greatest villain. Ikey Solomons was living out his last years in Hobart, Australia, having been transported there in 1831. His term was fourteen years but he would be released early in 1840. He would die in Hobart a decade later with little of the immense fortune he had once amassed. He was virtually anonymous at the time of his death, yet in his criminal prime he was called the Prince of Fences.

IKEY SOLOMONS

Isaac 'Ikey' Solomons was a slim man with dark skin, standing at 5ft 9in tall. He was born in the heart of Fagin country. His exact birthday and birthplace is contested, but the best guess is that he was born in 1785 in Gravel Lane. He was certainly born somewhere near Petticoat Lane. Very little is known about Solomons' early life and there are no certain facts about his childhood; but by the time he was in his early 20s he was a seasoned thief. By 1810 he had suffered his first arrest.

Solomons' arrest might have permanently nipped an illustrious criminal career in the bud. Along with a thief named Joel Joseph he had picked the pocket of a man named Thomas Dadd outside Westminster. There was a large crowd present as a meeting was in progress. Solomons was spotted. He tried to thread his way through Westminster Hall but the doors were fastened. Solomons and Joseph were trapped inside and captured. Ikey Solomons then found himself locked up in Newgate Gaol. He was put on trial at the Old Bailey. On 14 June 1810 Solomons and Joseph were sentenced to transportation for life.

Ikey Solomons. (Illustrated by Jean Nightingale)

Newgate Gaol, the eventual destination of Wild, Sheppard, Fagin and Ikey Solomons.

TRANSPORTATION

Long-term prison sentences as served in English penitentiaries were a thing of the future. If the authorities wanted to incarcerate a felon for an extended amount of time, they would transport them to the British colonies. The reason was very practical: prisoners were used as free labour. They were forced to do 'public works', i.e. building or domestic duties, or they were used as unpaid labour for 'free settlers'. The colonial regimes were often more brutal than even the primitive administrations of England's prisons, and whereas prisoners had been initially shipped off to the Americas, Australia was now the principal destination for those under sentence of transportation. Sentences tended to be given out in multiples of seven. Seven years, fourteen years, twenty-one years and life were the ascending scales of time doled out by the courts. Prisoners travelled to Australia in a fleet. The journey would take roughly eight months in overcrowded ships under debilitating conditions, with prisoners often in irons.

Prior to the voyage convicts were held in floating prisons called hulks. Hulks were old ships moored on either the Thames or the Medway.

Conditions on the hulks were often worse than those the convicts would experience on the ships that eventually transported them. Prisoners had to work on the hulks and their routine was hard. Solomons and Joseph's regime involved shifting timber and dredging the docks. The amount of time a prisoner would be forced to spend on a hulk before their voyage began could be variable in the extreme. Joel Joseph was removed from the hulks and sent to Australia in March 1811. Ikey Solomons spent six years waiting on the hulks to be transported. In January 1814 he was transferred from the hulk *Zealand* to the hulk *Retribution*.

THE PRINCE OF FENCES

At this point in his life, had Solomons been transported we might never have heard of him. But on 31 October 1816 the thief walked away from the *Retribution* a free man. His liberty was the consequence of a bizarre clerical accident combined with an atypical display of honesty on Solomons' part. There were two men named Solomons on the *Retribution*. The Secretary of State gave orders that the other Solomons was to be set free. On 15 July 1816 Ikey Solomons was released by accident. He enjoyed his liberty for a short while before giving himself up less than a month later. The authorities looked upon his gesture favourably and pardoned him.

There was a decade of silence. The historical vacuum has been filled with myths and rumours of Solomons' re-acquaintance with and ascendancy within the underworld. His apocryphal curriculum vitae was believed to have included time as a pimp, a moneylender, a conman, a burglar, a smuggler, a distributor of pornographic material and a kidsman. We do know that when Ikey Solomons re-emerged into recorded history, he was a very successful and wealthy receiver of stolen goods. His wife and children were also fully involved as co-workers within his empire. The geographical spine of his domain was Petticoat Lane. His home and headquarters were located nearby, on Bell's Lane in Spitalfields. Solomons had done well. His wealth was enormous but it would eventually attract the attention of the authorities.

In December 1825 a warehouse in the City of London was robbed and £200 worth of property was stolen. Charles Strachen, one of the owners of the warehouse, conducted a private investigation which cast suspicion on Ikey Solomons. Strachen obtained a warrant to search Ikey's Bell's Lane property. Some stolen items were found and a further warrant was issued for Ikey's arrest. Solomons went to ground but carried on operating. He was living in Islington using the alias Mr Jones but was recognised by a police officer. On 23 April 1827 he was arrested for the second time.

ESCAPE

While in custody, Ikey's lodgings were searched and more stolen property was retrieved. Victims of theft were encouraged to view the stolen items and determine whether any of it belonged to them. Solomons faced another trial at the Old Bailey and the prospect of another hefty punishment. Prior to the trial, Solomons was once again remanded at Newgate Gaol. He made an application for bail, which was a forlorn hope given his reputation. But the application necessitated a journey from Newgate to Westminster's law courts. As it turned out, Solomons' submission involved two trips to Westminster and during the second trip he escaped from custody.

On his journeys to and from Westminster Ikey was placed in a coach with two guards. The application for bail was rejected and Solomons was taken back to Newgate. When the coach reached Petticoat Lane, Solomons bounded out on to the street and lost himself in the neighbourhood he was intimately familiar with. The authorities couldn't find him.

Like many of Solomons' escapades, what actually happened is open to discussion. Differing accounts of the story have Ikey either convincing his guards

The Old Bailey. (Mark Nightingale)

to stop off at various pubs and pick up his wife, who subsequently faked a fit allowing Ikey to flee in the confusion; or have Ikey drugging the guards; or alternatively employing his father-in-law as the coach driver. Whatever the truth, Ikey was free and at large. A £50 reward was posted for his capture.

His family fared less well, however. His wife Ann was arrested when over £4,000 worth of stolen property was found in her house. His son John and his brother Benjamin were also arrested. All of them were found guilty. John and Benjamin received relatively light punishments, while Ann was sentenced to fourteen years' transportation. On 24 February 1828 she set sail on the *Mermaid* for Van Diemen's Land, taking six of her children with her.

VAN DIEMEN'S LAND

After the dramatic steps Ikey Solomons had taken to avoid imprisonment, what he did next was completely unexpected. Solomons missed his wife and exiled children, so he decided to go and join them in Van Diemen's Land. Little is known of his voyage to the Antipodes other than that he definitely sailed from Rio de Janeiro on a ship called the *Coronet*. He arrived in Van Diemen's Land on 10 July 1828.

Ann Solomons' predicament wasn't as bad as it could have been. She was a servant in the household of Richard Newman, an employee of Josiah Spode, the chief police magistrate. Three of her children had been placed in an orphanage in Hobart but three were permitted to live with her. Relations with her master and his wife were good. When Ikey arrived he was allowed to live with Ann, with the Newmans' approval. Richard Newman understood who Ikey Solomons was but kept the information from his superior officer.

Ikey's advent either coincided with, or else triggered, a breakdown in relations between Ann and the Newmans. A dispute quickly escalated over money and naturally there were multiple versions of the disagreement. Ikey Solomons claimed that Mr and Mrs Newman, under the assumption that he had means, had tapped him for a loan. There was also talk of John Newman's wife having slapped Ann across the face. The Newmans blamed the deterioration of their once cordial relationship with Ann on Ikey. Ann suffered the most in the crossfire when she was reassigned to a factory in Hobart.

Considering he was a fugitive, Ikey Solomons took the extraordinary step of getting the law involved. He told the chief of police who he was and lobbied the authorities to get Ann released into his custody. He was tenacious. He suffered setbacks but he got his way. He was eventually reunited with his wife, though it cost him a £1,000 bond to guarantee her good behaviour. He acquired property and set up a business. The amazing thing about the whole affair was that all and sundry seemed to be wilfully ignoring the elephant in the room, the blatant fact that Ikey Solomons was still a wanted man.

Solomons' fugitive status could not be ignored forever. The official reason for the colonial authorities in Van Diemen's Land's inertia regarding Solomons was the absence of formal proof that Solomons was who London authorities said he was. Nevertheless, London wanted him back. They sent official documentation, namely six warrants of commitment, to Van Diemen's Land. The documents arrived on 13 November 1829. Ikey Solomons was arrested. He made an application for a writ of habeas corpus and a complicated legal battle ensued. Ikey lost.

AN UNHAPPY ENDING

On 25 January 1830 Ikey Solomons sailed back to England as a prisoner. On 27 June he was locked up for the third time in Newgate Gaol and he stood trial at the Old Bailey. He was convicted on two counts of receiving stolen goods. In the criminal farce that had become Ikey Solomons' life, having evaded capture, avoided a transportation sentence and then voluntarily made his way to where he was probably going be transported anyway, only to be rearrested and sent back to London, Solomons was sentenced to fourteen years' transportation. He was shipped back to Van Diemen's Land on the convict vessel *William Glen Anderson*.

The voyage was not uneventful. Two convicts plotted a mutiny and Solomons informed on them. He arrived in Hobart on 1 November 1831 and, possibly as a reward for his part in quashing the mutiny, the job to which he was assigned was good. Solomons worked as an official in Richmond Gaol; but the period of favour didn't last long. Solomons got into trouble for using 'abusive language' and 'preferring false and malicious charges' towards a Mr I.G. McNeilly. Solomons kept his administrative job but was transferred to the more severe post of Port Arthur.

The downturn in Solomons' fortunes mirrored his domestic life. His beloved wife, for whom he had risked so much, was not particularly pleased to see him. Ann Solomons was now romantically involved with a free settler named George Madden. Ikey and Ann's relationship was a downward spiral of acrimony from that point on. Bad relations extended to his son David, who at one point physically attacked his father. Both Ikey and Ann got into further trouble with the authorities: Ikey for a drunken domestic incident, Ann for using abusive language. Yet in spite of this, both Ikey and Ann eventually received 'tickets of leave', a form of parole that permitted transported felons freedom of movement and certain civil liberties. Ann remarried in May 1841.

That same month Ikey and Ann were granted conditional pardons; they were effectively free. But Ikey Solomons was a spent force and had been for some time. He would never return to England and would die with around £70 in assets. It was not an immodest sum in itself, but it was a fraction of the fortune he had once commanded back in Petticoat Lane where he had reigned as the Prince of Fences.

FAGIN & IKEY SOLOMONS

Ikey Solomons and Fagin share ethnicity: both men were receivers of stolen goods; their stomping ground was more or less the same; they were both locked up in Newgate and tried in the Old Bailey. But there the similarities largely end. Solomons' tenure as a kidsman has no substance beyond the tall tales that substitute for facts in the years in which documented accounts of his activities are absent. There is no evidence that Solomons was as ruthless or violent as Fagin. Solomons bore no real physical resemblance to Fagin. Charles Dickens makes no mention of him in any surviving correspondence, and any reader would be hard pressed to find a reference to Ikey Solomons from any of the great Dickens biographers. Yet such is the potency of Solomons' example that he still continues to be linked with Dickens' great villain to this day.

5

THE MAN WHO KILLED SHERLOCK HOLMES

A VICTORIAN SUCCESS STORY

Given the supreme place of honour afforded to Sherlock Holmes in the canon of crime literature, it is interesting to note that Holmes didn't initially gel with the reading public. Sherlock Holmes made his debut in *Beeton's Christmas Album for 1887*. The adventure was 'A Study in Scarlet' which was published in novel form the following year. Its author, Arthur Conan Doyle, was paid a modest £25. The impact on the British reading public was hardly

The Great Detective Sherlock Holmes.
(Photographed by Mark Nightingale)

earth-shattering, yet *A Study in Scarlet* earned enough in its reprint edition to warrant a follow-up. Holmes returned in 1890 in *The Sign of Four*. A year later Doyle was asked to contribute a Holmes short story to a monthly periodical named *The Strand*. It would be Holmes' repeated appearances in *The Strand* that would provide the beginnings of a phenomenon that would make Doyle wealthy, world famous, and so umbilically identified with his creation that he would try to kill him.

As a young man Doyle studied medicine in Edinburgh. He published his first short story in *Chamber's Journal* when he was a student. A year after his graduation Doyle was practising medicine in Plymouth. He began writing in earnest during the hiatus between patients. As a youth Doyle was in awe of Edgar Allen Poe's 'Auguste Dupin' crime stories, in particular *The Murders in the Rue Morgue*. As an adult Doyle sought to build on the groundwork laid by Poe and write a novel-length crime story using the template provided by his hero.

DUPIN & A NEW TYPE OF DETECTIVE

Poe's Dupin is a supremely intelligent amateur detective who solves complex crimes, drawing astonishing conclusions via a highly attuned deductive reading of his environment. Dupin's motivation for solving a crime has as much to do with the recreational exercising of his mind as with redressing a wrong. The Dupin stories are set in an exotic and dangerous Paris. Dupin is several steps ahead of an unimaginative police force, and his adventures are narrated by an anonymous and admiring companion. Dupin is an uncompromising rationalist. The crime at the heart of *The Murders in the Rue Morgue* is a locked room double murder; a grotesque puzzle that almost implies a supernatural assailant. Dupin rejects such phantasmagorical possibilities. The conclusion of the mystery is earthbound (albeit pleasingly over the top).

Doyle's new creation and the criminal landscape he occupied expanded and fleshed out everything that Poe had sketched in his seminal crime stories. In actuality, Doyle improved on Poe. Holmes was a complex mixture of ascetic and decadent. Holmes' companion and chronicler Doctor Watson was more of a comic/dramatic foil/conscience to Doyle's creation than Dupin's companion ever was, and eminently more three-dimensional. The crimes Holmes investigated skilfully straddled the gap between the outrageous and the plausible. And Doyle's fictional London established itself in millions of readers' imaginations as the definitive gas-lit, smog-bound, late nineteenth-century metropolis.

If Doyle made any mistakes in the first two Sherlock Holmes novels it was his sparing use of Holmes. In both *A Study in Scarlet* and *The Sign of*

Four, Holmes disappears from large chunks of the plot as extended flashbacks form virtual novellas within the narrative. The novels are generally considered weaker for his absence. The short stories made no such mistake and Holmes became the centre of things.

THE STRAND

Holmes made his *Strand* debut in July 1891 in two stories: *A Scandal in Bohemia* and *The Red-Headed League*. The new magazine was only seven months old. Based on a format that was popular in America, *The Strand* was reasonably cheap to buy and sought to capitalise on the emerging middle-class market. Its content was a mixture of interviews, articles, illustrations, photographs and fiction. Initially, the fiction was imported from Europe. The Sherlock Holmes stories changed that; the public loved them.

Holmes' great editorial champion, Herbert Greenhough Smith, was the first to spot the creative and commercial mileage of the stories and encouraged Doyle to write more. Doyle obliged; by June 1892 he had written enough stories for a collection to be published the same year. The result was *The Adventures of Sherlock Holmes*. The success of the stories either in magazine or volume form sent readers back to the neglected novels. There was a demand for fresh Holmes material. A phenomenon had begun. The problem was that Doyle did not share his readership's love for his own creation. Doyle wanted to create literary art and he did not believe that the Holmes stories were particularly artistic. His output had always been varied and Doyle put more stock in his historical romances and works for the theatre than he ever did in the Holmes stories. As the demand for Holmes increased, Doyle began to nurse a serious grudge against his own creation.

Doyle initially tried to price himself out of the market. He asked *The Strand* for £1,000 for the next batch of Holmes stories. *The Strand* agreed and Doyle was committed to write them. But if he had to write more Holmes, then he determined that the final story would be the last one in which the detective would ever appear. Doyle decided to kill Holmes off. In truth, he had been consoling himself with the idea of killing Holmes for a while. The question now was the method of dispatch. Although Doyle relished the prospect of ridding himself of Holmes, he still had enough dramatic acumen and respect for the storytelling process to, at the very least, give Holmes a good death.

THE DEATH OF SHERLOCK HOLMES

In the summer of 1893 Arthur Conan Doyle was in Lucerne, Switzerland, on a speaking engagement, when he struck up a friendship with a small group of English clergymen. Doyle enjoyed their company and went on walks with them through the spectacular Swiss countryside. He unburdened himself regarding his frustrations with Holmes and his desire to kill him off. At some point during one of their walks, Doyle and company found themselves by the waterfall at Reichenbach. The path leading up to the waterfall was narrow; the drop was sheer; the waterfall itself was primal. It was suggested that if Doyle was still intent on killing Holmes, then the waterfall might well provide a suitable graveyard for him. The idea lodged itself in Doyle's mind. He had the ending for his story. What he needed now was a suitable antagonist to send Holmes to his death. The story that heralded Holmes' exit was *The Final Problem*.

In the story, Watson is surprised by the unexpected appearance of Holmes at his house. Holmes, who is supposed to have been in France, looks drawn and exhibits the physical wear and tear of having been in a fight. Holmes wants to leave the country for a while and implores Watson to come with him. Holmes asks Watson if he has ever heard of Professor Moriarty. Watson hasn't. Holmes gives Watson a brief history of the professor: Moriarty comes from a good family. He is extremely gifted academically, having written a paper on Binomial Theorem at only 21 years of age. He won 'the mathematical chair at one of our smaller universities' but resigned under an unspecified cloud of rumour. He moved to London where he became thoroughly ensconced in respectable society. But the reality is that Moriarty is the dark heart of criminal London, controlling and organising every significant professional criminal enterprise in the capital. Holmes calls Moriarty 'the Napoleon of crime' and likens him to a spider at the centre of an enormous web. Moriarty is completely insulated from detection and suspicion. Holmes has been investigating Moriarty and his organisation, looking for a means by which to bring him down. Holmes was initially unsuccessful but has eventually managed to capitalise on a rare mistake Moriarty has made. This proves opportunity enough for Holmes to build a case against him and his cohorts, solid enough to bring the arch-criminal and his empire to an end. There is a problem, however. Holmes has a time constraint. He can only implement his plan in three days' time but Holmes must be physically present in London for the plan to work and Moriarty is fully aware of what Holmes plans to do.

Holmes relays the events leading directly up to his appearance at Watson's house. Earlier that day Moriarty had visited Holmes in person. The conversation was polite but Moriarty heavily implied that should Holmes make his final move against him, the only action left available to the professor would

Holmes leaves 221B Baker Street and is pursued across London by Moriarty's assassins. (Mark Nightingale)

On the corner of Bentick Street and Welbeck Street, Holmes is almost trampled to death by a two-horse van. (Mark Nightingale)

be to have Holmes killed. Holmes stood his ground and Moriarty made his exit. Holmes left his apartment in Baker Street and journeyed on foot across London to Watson's house. Three attempts were made on his life: he was nearly run down by a two-horse van on the corner of Bentick and Welbeck Street; he narrowly avoided being crushed by falling bricks on Vere Street, after which he found brief sanctuary in Pall Mall at his brother Mycroft's home; then as he made his way to Watson's house he was attacked by a thug with a bludgeon.

London is now no longer safe. Holmes makes his plans to leave the country and arranges to meet Watson at Victoria Station the following day.

Holmes and Watson escape from London in an elaborate cat and mouse chase. Holmes narrowly eludes Moriarty at Victoria and Watson learns that Moriarty has had Holmes' apartment at Baker Street set on fire. Moriarty charters a private train and the chase extends across the English countryside. Holmes and Watson cross the Channel, travel through France and rest for a while in Brussels.

News reaches Holmes from England that Moriarty's gang have been broken up but Moriarty has escaped. Holmes fears retribution and implores Watson to leave him. Watson refuses. Holmes and Watson continue their travels through Switzerland. They arrive at the village of Meiringen, where they go for a trip across the hills to see the waterfall at Riechenbach. A messenger from their hotel arrives calling Watson back to tend to a dying English guest.

Watson is reluctant to leave Holmes but is duty-bound to go. Yet the message is false. When Watson returns to Reichenbach as fast as he can, Holmes is nowhere to be found. The nearby ground reveals evidence of a struggle. Two sets of footprints disappear off the edge of the precipice. Watson finds some of Holmes' personal belongings near the cliff's edge. Among them is a note. In the note Holmes describes his final meeting with Moriarty who has given him permission to write to Watson. Holmes relays some final particulars about the case and says his last farewell to his old friend.

Watson deduces that the two men, shortly after the letter's completion, fought one another and then fell to their deaths.

THE FINAL PROBLEM

The Final Problem is not a particularly subtle story. It has the feel of something written well but written in haste. There is a sense of Doyle quickly winding up his affairs regarding Holmes. In the opening paragraph, Watson mentions by name A Study in Scarlet and The Naval Treaty, Holmes' first and penultimate adventures in print. Doyle even destroys Holmes' base of operations at Baker Street. For a detective series in which a large element of the pleasure is derived from Holmes solving impossible puzzles, there is a large irony at work in The Final Problem. This last story has Holmes pitched against his most intelligent adversary, but has him do no visible detective work. Holmes talks about his investigations into Moriarty's network but the reader never finds out what Holmes does or how he actually manages to incriminate Moriarty. It is as if Doyle can't be bothered with the time it would take to explain these things. He just wants to kill Holmes.

This sense of urgency works in the story's favour as The Final Problem is essentially an action story, one of the best ever written. London, always potent in Doyle's work, is particularly alive during the two chase sequences, as first Holmes, and then Holmes and Watson, are hunted through its streets by Moriarty and his criminal army. But The Final Problem is also very strong on character. Holmes and Watson, the head and the heart of the series, are as beautifully crafted as ever. Their friendship is believable, complex and moving. And in trying to find a suitable murder weapon with which to finish off Sherlock Holmes for good, Arthur Conan Doyle constructs one of literatures greatest villains.

MORIARTY

Holmes describes Moriarty like this:

He is extremely tall and thin, his forehead domes out in a white curve, and his two eyes are deeply sunken in his head. He is clean-shaven, pale, and ascetic-looking, retaining something of the professor in his features. His shoulders are rounded from much study, and his face protrudes forward, and is forever oscillating from side to side in a curiously reptilian fashion. He peered at me with great curiosity in his puckered eyes.

He describes Moriarty's speech as having a 'soft, precise fashion of sincerity which a mere bully could not produce'.

Holmes and Moriarty's meeting at Baker Street is relatively polite, yet laced with implied threats and strained professional courtesy between two equals. It is an electrifying exchange and one of the great confrontations in crime

Professor James Moriarty. (Illustrated by Jean Nightingale)

fiction. Doyle's genius is in keeping Moriarty off the page for most of the narrative and revealing him through his effect on Holmes. Holmes clearly respects Moriarty. He admits that in Moriarty he has 'met an antagonist who was my intellectual equal. My horror at his crimes was lost in admiration for his skill.' Moriarty is clearly presented as a satanic inverse of Holmes (the physical description of Moriarty being not that dissimilar to that of Holmes himself). Moriarty's potential for good and Holmes' for corruption are each reflected in the other. Holmes sees the demolition of Moriarty's organisation as his greatest accomplishment.

The most shocking element in *The Final Problem* (apart from Holmes' death) is the level of fear and anxiety that Moriarty produces in Holmes. Throughout most of his adventures Holmes retains an unflappable command of his environment, but in *The Final Problem*, when Holmes first appears, Watson remarks how his appearance is 'paler and thinner than usual'. Holmes quickly admits to being afraid. He cannot guarantee his own or Watson's safety if they stay in London. Holmes' safety and Moriarty's destruction are ultimately dependent on Holmes running away; and when Holmes meets Moriarty face to face he does something extraordinary – he produces a cocked gun and lays it on the table in front of his enemy. It is an unprecedented manoeuvre for Sherlock Holmes. He fears for his life and appears to weigh up the possibility that he might be forced to shoot Moriarty dead. For a detective whose greatest weapon was always logic, it seems an admission of partial defeat for the deductive process in which he placed his absolute confidence. Two great minds had reached an impasse. The only logical dramatic resolution was violent conflict and death.

A GRADUAL RESURRECTION

With the publication of *The Final Problem*, Arthur Conan Doyle would have expected a backlash, but when the story appeared in the 1893 Christmas edition of *The Strand*, the public response was borderline hysteria. A colourful mythology has sprung up around the extremities of the public reaction to Holmes' death: Doyle was allegedly assaulted in the street by an angry woman wielding a handbag; clerks in the city were said to have worn funeral garments; royalty was even perceived to have been upset by Doyle's controversial decision. Whatever truth there is in these anecdotes, the public undoubtedly felt aggrieved. *The Strand* had a more practical reason to feel concerned. The commercial success of the magazine was inextricably linked to Sherlock Holmes. The publication of *The Final Problem* led to a disturbingly high number of readers abandoning the magazine now that Holmes could no longer be guaranteed within its pages. By the close of the century, *Strand* circulation had dropped alarmingly without Holmes as its main selling point. The pressure to bring him back was enormous and ever-present. But Doyle (publically at any rate) was defiant and flippantly dismissive of his decision to kill Holmes.

Doyle caved in, however, in increments. In 1897 he wrote a Sherlock Holmes play. He wrote it with the great Victorian actor Herbert Beerbohm Tree in mind. But Doyle was not resurrecting Holmes. The story was to take place prior to the events chronicled in *The Final Problem*. Moriarty would also appear in the play. Beerbohm Tree overextended himself by wanting to play both Holmes and Moriarty, and the project folded. The play was taken up by the New York producer Charles Frohman as a vehicle for the American actor Charles Gillette.[1] The script was dramatically revised, and the end result was an amalgam of the plots of three existing Sherlock Holmes stories, including *The Final Problem*.

The next stage in Doyle's drift back towards Holmes was his submission of two stories to *The Strand*: *The Man Who Watches* and *The Last Special*. Both were essentially Holmes stories in all but name.

In 1901 Doyle was toying with the idea of writing a mystery story centred around some Dartmoor myths he had heard his friend Bertram Fletcher Robinson talk about. But Doyle had a problem: the basic structure of the new story was sound, but there was a missing ingredient. Doyle had difficulty inventing a compelling detective to solve the mystery. There was an obvious solution. The writer had outmanoeuvred himself, creating a space in his own narrative that only Sherlock Holmes could satisfactorily fill. The story became *The Hound of the Baskervilles*. Holmes was back, after a fashion; but if Doyle submitted to the idea of writing an original Holmes story, he still drew the line at raising him from the dead. The events of *The Hound of the Baskervilles* were set before *The Final Problem*. Holmes was still at the bottom of Reichenbach and Doyle wanted him to stay there.

The Hound of the Baskervilles breathed fresh commercial life into the fortunes of *The Strand* when its serialisation began in August 1901. The novel was a huge success. However, if Doyle had intended *The Hound of the Baskervilles* to be a one-off concession to sate the appetites of fans who had applied half a decade's worth of pressure to bring Holmes back, he was badly mistaken. Doyle had made the mistake of writing an outstanding novel, the best remembered of all the Sherlock Holmes stories. The public wanted more. The publishing industry wanted more. Doyle was offered astronomical amounts of money by the American magazine *Colliers*, as well as favourable terms with *The Strand* for Holmes' permanent return. He finally caved in, having made a peace, of sorts, with his creation that would last the rest of his life. The initial challenge was how to resurrect Sherlock Holmes.

As it turned out, the solution was reasonably easy. In *The Final Problem*, Watson had not actually seen Holmes die. Holmes' body had never been recovered (lending weight to psychological theories that subconsciously Doyle had never intended to kill Holmes). The story that heralded Holmes' return from the dead was *The Empty House*. Doyle chose not to resurrect Professor Moriarty. His corpse (although never found) would remain forever at Reichenbach. But Doyle did reanimate Moriarty after a fashion. His malign influence hung over *The Empty House* as Holmes tackled the last high-ranking member of Moriarty's organisation still at large.

THE EMPTY HOUSE

Set three years after the events of *The Final Problem*, *The Empty House* begins with a violent murder. Faintly reminiscent of Doyle's beloved *Murders in the Rue Morgue*, *The Empty House* is a locked room mystery. The murder victim is Ronald Adair, a wealthy London gentleman. He is found dead in the upper room of his Park Lane property. The room has been locked from the inside and Adair's skull has been shattered by a pistol round. There is no evidence of suicide; nobody heard a gun being fired; nobody had entered the ground floor of the property. In the absence of Holmes, Watson attempts to investigate the crime. During his enquiries he encounters a deformed man. The man visits Watson at his home and requests an audience. He reveals himself as Sherlock Holmes in disguise. Watson faints. When Watson comes round, Holmes explains the circumstances of his apparent death.

At Reichenbach, shortly after finishing his letter to Watson, Holmes and Moriarty fight. Holmes narrowly bests Moriarty and pitches him over the cliff into the waters of Reichenbach. Holmes loses his balance and tips over the cliff, but saves himself from falling. In that moment Holmes makes the decision to allow the world at large to think him dead. His rationale is that a small number of his more powerful enemies are still at large. If they were to think him dead then they would become complacent and therefore easier to catch by the existing powers that be. Holmes watches Watson retrieve his letter but does not reveal himself. When Watson is gone, Holmes climbs back onto the path but is almost killed by a falling boulder dislodged by a hidden henchman of Moriarty's. Holmes flees and shows himself only to his brother Mycroft.[2]

Holmes observes from afar the demolition of Moriarty's organisation. He travels the world incognito visiting Persia, Mecca, Khartoum and France, all the time keeping an eye on his enemies in London. By the time of the Adair murder, only one man still poses a threat to Holmes. He is, of course, Adair's assassin. This is the same man who tried to kill Holmes at Reichenbach, the only member of Moriarty's gang to successfully evade capture. Holmes' intention is to bring the criminal to justice that evening.

In a stealthier variation of *The Final Problem*'s dash through London's streets, Watson and Holmes thread their way through 'a network of mews and stables', emerging at a 'small road lined with old, gloomy houses'. They pass through Manchester Street and Blandford Street, and enter the rear door of an empty house to which Holmes possesses a key. It is Camden House, situated opposite Holmes' old living quarters at 221b Baker Street.

Watson observes Holmes' silhouette in the window at Baker Street. The silhouette is a wax model that Holmes has had placed there as a decoy. Holmes and Watson wait in silence. A third man enters the house unaware of their presence. The stranger positions himself by the window opposite Holmes' wax decoy and assembles a customised high-power air rifle. He inserts a revolver bullet into the air rifle, takes aim and shoots the wax dummy. The gun makes no sound as it fires. Holmes and Watson confront the sniper and subdue him. The sniper is revealed to be the murderer of Ronald Adair. The motive for murder is relatively squalid. Adair and the assassin were gambling partners; the assassin had been cheating and had amassed a large amount of money, and Adair had found out and was about to expose him. The identity of the murderer is Colonel Sebastian Moran, Professor Moriarty's most valuable compatriot. Holmes, on his return to London, had allowed himself to be spotted by Moran's cohorts in order to provoke Moran into an attempt on his life.

MORAN

Colonel Moran is a terrific villain, arguably more colourful than Moriarty. Watson offers this physical description of him:

> He was an elderly man, with a thin projecting nose, a high, bald forehead, and a huge grizzled moustache ... His face was gaunt and swarthy, scored with deep and savage lines ... It was a tremendously virile and yet sinister face which was turned towards us. With the brow of a philosopher above and the jaw of a sensualist below, the man must have started with great capacities for good or for evil. But one could not look upon his cruel blue eyes, with their drooping, cynical lids, or upon the fierce, aggressive nose and the threatening, deep lined brow, without reading Nature's plainest danger signal.

The reader discovers that Moran has a respectable lineage and a good education by way of Eton and Oxford. He has a distinguished military career behind him, having served in India and Afghanistan. He is the author of a book on hunting. Moran is an outstanding shot and expert tiger hunter, his great colonial exploit being a crawl into a drain to kill a flesh-eating tiger that had taken refuge there. Holmes even draws the comparison between Moran's physical appearance and that of a tiger.

In fleshing out his new villainous creation, Doyle provides further insight into Moriarty and the administration of his criminal empire. Although dead, Moriarty lives on the page vicariously through Moran. Moran's withdrawal from India and his subsequent return to England provide the context in which Moran and Moriarty first meet. Moriarty effectively headhunts Moran for a high-ranking post in his organisation. Moran is employed for a season as Moriarty's chief of staff, but after a while the nature of his employment changes. Moriarty pays Moran a retainer and only uses him for specialised criminal assignments. Doyle is unspecific about what these assignments are, but murder appears to be one of them, Holmes citing the recent death of a Mrs Stewart as a possible Moran assassination. Moran is partial to unusual weaponry. The airgun he uses to kill Adair is commissioned by Moriarty and constructed by a blind German mechanic named Von Herder.

The fate of Moran is grim. Holmes' prognosis is that 'the bullets alone are enough to put his head in the noose'. Moran is destined for the gallows. But the tiger hunter and professional assassin achieves, along with Moriarty, a form of immortality. Although Doyle did not create the archetype of the master villain's dangerous and exotic henchman, he certainly invented one of the best examples in print. From that point on, every bodyguard with a grotesque appearance, an array of specialist skills and an arsenal of unusual weaponry, in crime, spy or pulp fiction, would owe something to Colonel Sebastian Moran, loyal and fanatical enforcer of Professor James Moriarty.

Colonel Sebastian Moran. (Illustrated by Stephen Dennis)

AFTERLIFE

Holmes was back. Doyle and Holmes were stuck with one another for the remainder of the author's life and career. Numerous short stories and a further novel would follow. Doyle had elected not to resurrect Moriarty. In fact, Doyle's retelling of Moriarty's death in *The Empty House* leaves little room for a possible return, as the criminal's elderly body is observed by Holmes to have 'struck a rock, bounced off and splashed into the water'. But the master villain's legacy would remain alive via periodic references in the stories that were to follow. *The Norwood Builder*, the story immediately following *The Empty House*, begins with a reference to Moriarty. Holmes complains that: 'From the point of view of the criminal expert ... London has become a singularly uninteresting city since the death of the late lamented Professor Moriarty.' Watson gently reproves Holmes for his short-term memory and lack of perspective, and Holmes' response betrays the strange symbiosis he shares with his arch-enemy: 'Well, well, I must not be selfish ... The community is certainly the gainer, and no one the loser, save the poor out-of-work specialist, whose occupation has gone.'

In *The Missing Three-Quarter*, Holmes observes that in Dr Leslie Armstrong he may have found a gentleman with the intellectual potential to 'fill the gap left by the illustrious Moriarty'. In *His Last Bow*, the defeated villain Von Bork swears that he will take revenge on Holmes. Holmes invokes the memory of both Moriarty and Moran in his riposte, referring to Von Bork's threats as 'The Old Sweet Song ... How often I have heard it in days gone by. It was a favourite ditty of the late lamented Professor Moriarty. Colonel Sebastian Moran has also been known to warble it.'

Doyle's final reference to Moriarty in the short stories is in *The Adventures of the Illustrious Client*. A prospective employer refers to a potential opponent of both Holmes and Watson as 'the most dangerous man in Europe'. Holmes uses the example of Moriarty to provide a degree of perspective to his client's hyperbole: 'I have had several opponents to whom that flattering term has been applied ... If your man is more dangerous than Professor Moriarty ... then he is indeed worth meeting.' Holmes also includes Moran in his hierarchy of dangerous criminality, revealing that Moran, rather than being hanged as Holmes prophesied, is still alive (and presumably rotting in prison).[3]

Moriarty had one final part to play in Holmes' tangled chronology. In 1914 the final Sherlock Holmes novel was serialised in *The Strand*. Anticipation for the novel was immense. The magazine marked the event with the first colour illustrations used in a Sherlock Holmes adventure. The title of the story was *The Valley of Fear*. It was set before the events of *The Final Problem* and afforded Professor Moriarty the opportunity to reappear.

THE VALLEY OF FEAR

The Valley of Fear begins with Holmes in the middle of a detailed investigation into Moriarty's criminal fraternity, for which he has managed to place a man on the inside. The informer's identity is secret but he communicates with Holmes under the alias of 'Porlock'. Holmes receives a coded letter from Porlock, in which Porlock expresses concern that he is close to being discovered. The informer also conveys a warning to Holmes that a certain Douglas of Birlstone Manor's life is in danger. Holmes is visited by Inspector MacDonald of Scotland Yard, who announces that a John Douglas of Birlstone Manor has been murdered that morning, blasted in the face with a shotgun round. MacDonald requires Holmes' assistance. Holmes discerns Moriarty's hand in Douglas' death. He believes the murder to be either a revenge killing for disloyalty or else a contract murder, 'engineered by Moriarty in the ordinary course of business'.

The first part of *The Valley of Fear* deals with Holmes' investigation into the Douglas murder. The killing is resolved reasonably quickly in seven chapters. Douglas' murderer turns out to be Douglas himself – the dead body is actually that of an assassin sent after him. As the face of the corpse has been obliterated by shotgun fire, Douglas disguises the body to make it look as if he was the victim. The majority of the rest of the narrative tells John Douglas' story.

Douglas is, in reality, a Pinkerton detective named Birdy Edwards. His investigations into an American criminal organisation called the 'Scowrers' forms the bulk of the novel. Edwards breaks up the main body of the gang, but there are enough disparate elements still at large to ensure that he will be a marked man unless drastic action is taken. Edwards relocates to England and reinvents himself as John Douglas.

In the epilogue we discover that Douglas has been cleared of murder. Holmes deduces (although he cannot prove it) that Moriarty has been approached by the Scowrers – and Douglas' death had been subcontracted to Moriarty. Having failed to kill Douglas, Moriarty's reputation in the underworld is at stake. Further attempts on John Douglas' life are therefore inevitable. Holmes cannot guarantee Douglas' safety and compels him to leave the country. Two months later, Holmes receives a letter. The letter is unsigned but contains the sentences 'Dear me, Mr. Holmes! Dear me!' Shortly afterwards, Holmes learns that Douglas is dead, drowned in an apparent accident off the coast of St Helena.

The Valley of Fear is traditionally regarded as the least of Doyle's four Sherlock Holmes novels, and it is not hard to understand why. There are chronological inconsistencies. In *The Final Problem* Watson hears about Moriarty for the first time. In *The Empty House* Watson hears about Colonel

Moran for the first time. *The Valley of Fear* is set before the events of *The Final Problem* and Watson is lectured in detail about the workings of Moriarty and, to a lesser extent, Moran. This is a glaring error but a consistent problem in the Sherlock Holmes stories.[4] In *The Valley of Fear* the unforgivable sin Doyle commits is once again that of sidelining Sherlock Holmes for the majority of the novel. In terms of *The Valley of Fear*'s contribution to Holmes mythology, the first seven chapters and the epilogue are the most important elements. These sections of the book act as an extended lecture on Moriarty and could almost be mistaken for an encyclopaedia entry on everything alluded to in *The Final Problem*.

Moriarty never physically appears in *The Valley of Fear*, yet this novel provides more detailed information about him and his organisation than all the other stories that either feature or mention him. Doyle regurgitates the same comparisons between Moriarty and Napoleon, and Moriarty and a spider, that he had used to great effect in *The Final Problem*. In fact, Doyle goes slightly mad with animal metaphors, likening Moriarty to a shark, a jackal and a lion. Holmes makes constant references to Moriarty's intelligence. He is 'one of the first brains in Europe', 'a great brain in London' and 'the most famous scientific criminal'. As an academic, Moriarty is revealed to be the author of the esteemed scientific text *The Dynamics of an Asteroid*. He is insulated by respectable society, unsuspected and untouchable. Inspector MacDonald (who, unlike Holmes at this point, has actually met Moriarty) even describes the professor's physical touch in ecclesiastical terms, 'like a father's blessing'.

We learn fresh biographical detail about Moriarty. He is a bachelor and his brother is a station master. Holmes has, on three separate occasions, been in his empty office. He has found nothing directly incriminating but reports the presence of a painting called *La Jeune Fille a l'Agneau* by Jean Baptiste Greuze. The painting is worth approximately £4,000. Moriarty's legitimate salary is £700 a year. Owning a painting he can't possibly afford provides the link by which Holmes explains to MacDonald how Moriarty's finances work. Moriarty has twenty bank accounts spread across six banks, 'the bulk of his fortune abroad in the Deutsch'. We even find out how much Colonel Moran is paid (£6,000 per year – a higher wage than the prime minister).

Doyle reiterates the vast scope of Moriarty's empire and the ethos by which he controls it. Moriarty's gang is described rather poetically as 'one hundred broken fighting men, with every sort of crime in between'. Moriarty governs 'with a rod of iron over his people. His discipline is tremendous. There is only one punishment in his code. It is death.'

While the early Moriarty sections in *The Valley of Fear* are useful for fleshing out the master villain and his criminal institution, they are a little overwritten and come close to parodying their equivalent passages in *The Final Problem*.

Holmes, in describing Moriarty, often comes across like an alliterative music hall master of ceremonies. The epilogue is another matter. Sinister and economic, Moriarty's only recorded words in *The Valley of Fear* are chilling in their deliberately quaint assertion of victory over Holmes. Up until that point, Holmes' attitude towards Moriarty has been relatively playful. He is not yet afraid of the professor. Their contest is still a game to Holmes. By the close of *The Valley of Fear*, Holmes' fixation on Moriarty is no longer a game. Holmes begins to show signs of the fear that will colour his dealings with Moriarty in *The Final Problem*. Holmes' last words in the novel express a rare doubt in his own abilities: 'I do not say he can't be beat ... But you must give me time Watson — you must give me time.' *The Valley of Fear* is less a novel than an adjunct to the primal battle between Holmes and Moriarty; a fight that will rage across London and end at Reichenbach.

Arthur Conan Doyle's reinvention of the master criminal provided a sort of ground zero for fictional villainy. From that point on, in terms of a villain's genius, the ubiquity and omniscience of their empire, the complexity of their criminal enterprise, the duality of their relationship with their archenemy, and their employment of dangerous henchmen, multiplied villains from fiction and pulp fiction would owe more to the Moriarty template than any of the professor's fictional antecedents. And in trying to rid himself of the burden of Holmes, Doyle had created a villain so potent that he would doubly ensure that Doyle was handcuffed to Holmes and the universe he had created for time immemorial.

Moriarty was a creature born principally out of Doyle's imagination. As far as real inspirations were concerned, Doyle name checks Jonathan Wild as one historical inspiration for the 'Napoleon of Crime'. But there was another more contemporary model for Moriarty — the London-based American gang boss Adam Worth.

6

Little Adam & The Eye

Suspects

There are many people from Arthur Conan Doyle's wide and varied circle of friends, associates and contemporaries that can claim to have inspired Professor Moriarty. Doyle was at school with a mathematician named James Moriarty. A criminal called George Moriarty made the papers in 1874. But apart from having a colourful surname that Arthur Conan Doyle may have utilised, there was little about George Moriarty that prefigured Doyle's creation. George was a petty criminal. He was violent and an alcoholic. He would have scarcely caused a ripple had it not been for his unstable and erratic behaviour in court, which included trying to throw himself through the court house window. George Moriarty was far too stupid and incompetent to have provided Doyle with any more than an interesting surname for his villain.

Doyle may have culled Moriarty's formidable mathematical abilities and expertise regarding the dynamics of asteroids from his associate Major-General Drayson. Moriarty's physicality might have been borrowed from James Payne, the editor of *The Cornhill Magazine*. Doyle loved the works of Robert Louis Stevenson and Stevenson's novel *Jekyll and Hyde* might well have cast its shadow over Doyle's creation. The historic inspiration for Stevenson's monster was the Scottish burglar Deacon Brodie (a respectable gentleman by day and vicious criminal by night), who lived a similar double existence to Doyle's professor.

Doyle was believed to have furnished Moriarty with qualities he personally disliked. He hated mathematics, therefore Moriarty became a mathematician. Doyle disliked the Irish, so it stood to reason that although Moriarty could pass himself off as a respectable Englishman, Irish blood flowed through his veins.

There was one extraordinary figure from Doyle's youth who may have provided dual inspiration for both Sherlock Holmes and Professor Moriarty. Sir Robert Christison was an ancient fixture at Edinburgh University when Doyle was a medical student. Christison was something of a legend. He was Professor of Materia Medica and Therapeutics. He had championed the cause of pharmacology, changing the academic priorities of the university to favour his discipline. He wrote two seminal publications: *A Treatise on Poisons* and *Medico-Lego Examination of Dead Bodies*. He was obsessed with the toxic properties of plants and poisons to the point of sometimes conducting risky experiments on himself. In the course of his long life, Christison nearly killed himself by ingesting poison during such an experiment. Quick thinking saved him. He drank his own shaving water, which induced a vomiting fit that dumped the lethal toxins on the floor. Christison took cocaine. He climbed a mountain in his old age, his body fortified by the drug. But Christison's great feat occurred early in his career, when his medical evidence helped secure convictions against the infamous Edinburgh grave robbers Burke and Hare.

All of the above were eminently Holmesian qualities, but Christison had a dark side and a dual nature: he was arguably a misogynist; he was nepotistic; his system of advancing those he favoured within the academic community was deemed underhand and nefarious. While these are undoubtedly unpleasant qualities, they are not really satanic enough to put him in the forefront of Moriarty templates. Doyle biographer Andrew Lycett holds Christison up as a serious contender for the man who inspired Moriarty, but common consensus bestows that honour on a remarkable nineteenth-century American thief named Adam Worth.

BEGINNINGS

Adam Worth was born in Germany in 1844. When he was 5 years old his mother and father moved to America. The family settled in Cambridge, Massachusetts. Worth ran away from home when he was 14. He went to Boston and then on to New York, where he got a job as a clerk. Apart from interim periods when he worked for his father, Worth's flirtation with legitimate employment lasted just one month.

When the American Civil War began, Worth enlisted in the Federal Army. Although soldiering constituted legal employment, at 17 Adam Worth was too young to fight. He lied about his age. He was unusually short (and would acquire the nickname 'Little Adam') but was inducted into the army nevertheless. On enlisting, Worth was paid a handsome bounty of $1,000 (a recruitment incentive common at the beginning of the Civil War). Worth joined the 34th Light Artillery. As a soldier he must have shown some aptitude because he was rapidly promoted to corporal and then sergeant. He saw action very quickly in one of the first pitch battles of the war. As one of the bloodiest engagements in American history, the Battle of Bull Run was Worth's first induction into the realities of violence. He was injured and hospitalised. He was reported as killed, but he recovered from his injuries and took advantage of the confusion regarding his casualty status. He deserted and re-enlisted under a different name, collecting another hefty bounty. Worth was now a professional 'bounty jumper', his first successful criminal enterprise. He was caught but was not particularly well guarded; he escaped and carried on bounty jumping. He even changed sides and bounty jumped amongst the ranks of his former Southern enemies. When the war was over, Adam Worth made his way back to New York and tried his hand at crime.

APPRENTICESHIP

For Adam Worth, aged 20, the possibilities for criminal advancement in the New York of the 1860s were legion. From top to bottom the city was corrupt. The police department and City Hall were institutionally crooked, while a more flagrant and primitive criminality ruled at ground level and numerous bizarrely named gangs controlled the streets in the poorer areas of the metropolis. Adam Worth began his New York apprenticeship as a pickpocket. He proved himself a skilled thief and before long commanded a small gang. He showed great aptitude for organising crimes. He was also a keen observer of the criminal landscape around him and came very quickly to conclusions that would serve him throughout his long career. Brutality surrounded him and Worth quickly surmised that violence was counter-productive to good criminal business practice. He determined not to use it unless absolutely necessary. Neither would he employ criminals for whom violence was a first recourse. Worth also saw the virtues in not getting too personally involved with the implementation of the crimes he had planned. He was, however, to periodically break this rule throughout his career, with damaging consequences.

In 1864 Adam Worth was arrested. He had been caught stealing and was sentenced to three years' hard labour in Sing Sing Gaol. Worth served one week of his sentence and escaped. Taking advantage of a change in the guard, he took refuge in a ditch, swam across the Hudson River to a barge, hid inside the barge and waited while it was towed back to the city. Imprisonment was a temporary setback; Worth was on the ascendance. He clearly had the makings of a great thief – all he needed was patronage. Mentorship came in the form of the corpulent Grand Dame of the New York underworld, 'Marm' Mandelbaum. As the most respected handler of stolen goods in the city, Mandelbaum was one of its most connected villains. She occupied a dual position of prominence in the underworld and respectable society. She plotted and organised great crimes and her favour and good will was tantamount to promotion in the underworld. Mandelbaum was everything Worth aspired to be, and she nurtured a soft spot for the young thief.

In the swarm of criminals that prospered in Mandelbaum's orbit, Worth met his great partner in crime, as well as a future enemy, in the forms of 'Piano' Charley Bullard and Max 'the Baron' Shinburn. Piano Charley was a skilled burglar. He was also a gifted musician, a womaniser, gambler and drinker. Shinburn was a very good bank burglar and an inventor of safe-cracking devices. He was also treacherous and a terrible snob with delusions of aristocracy. When Piano Charley was arrested, Worth and Shinburn broke him out. Piano Charley's liberation cemented a professional and filial bond between himself and Worth. Worth immediately distanced himself from Shinburn and the two men (who never really liked each other from the offset) went their separate ways, both nurturing a lifelong antipathy that would have debilitating consequences for Worth in years to come.

In the mid to late 1860s Worth organised a string of robberies: he took $20,000 worth of bonds in the Cambridge Robbery; he took $100,000 from the Merchants Union and Express Company; and he attempted to rob the Atlantic Transportation Company, yet failed. But in 1869 Adam Worth conducted the most celebrated crime he ever committed on American soil.

GRADUATION

Adam Worth targeted the Boylston National Bank in Boston. He rented the property next door to the bank and set up a bogus business, a tonic shop. He filled the shop window with a gigantic display of tonic bottles, the purpose of which was twofold. It presented a legitimate business facade but also prevented anybody from being able to see what was actually going on inside the shop. Inside, Adam Worth, Piano Charley Bullard and a third man were digging through the side of the shop wall into the bank. It took the thieves a week to reach the Boylston vault and crack open the bank's safe. Estimates vary as to how much they took, but it may have been as much as $1 million.

Worth's crime was one of the most spectacular robberies ever committed in an American metropolis. It was bold, outrageous and some newspapers could barely hide the admiration they felt for the criminal chutzpah on display. Worth's crime became an international talking point.

The majority of the haul took the form of bonds. Worth probably intended to sell the bonds back to the bank at something less than their actual value. The bank more than likely would comply, and Worth and company would still walk away with a fortune. But this would take time to organise and Adam Worth didn't have that much time to spare. There was a concerted manhunt for the men responsible and America was becoming too dangerous a country to remain in. Worth was in danger of becoming a victim of his own success. He left the bonds with sympathetic lawyers who would cautiously open up the necessary channels of communication with the bank. In the meantime, he needed to leave the country for a while and occupy himself until the deal was struck and the money made its way back to him. Adam Worth and Piano Charley Bullard assumed false identities and boarded a steamer for Liverpool.

KITTY

In 1870 Worth and Piano Charley arrived in Liverpool on the SS *Indiana*. They masqueraded as Texas oilmen. Their respective noms de plume were Henry J. Raymond and Charles H. Wells. They made the Washington Hotel their temporary base of operations. Tending bar at the Washington was a 17-year-old named Kitty Flynn. Kitty was Irish. She was smart, passionate and aspirational. She had left a dirt-poor childhood in Dublin behind her, and the sight of two flamboyant Americans with a cavalier attitude towards spending money attracted her attention. Worth and Bullard were equally enchanted by Flynn. Before long the three adventurers were seeing each other regularly. Flynn was courted and bedded by both Bullard and Worth. They shared Kitty between them, each with the full knowledge of the other. Kitty was perfectly happy with the arrangement, and within a very short space of time she even married Bullard. Marriage didn't stop Kitty sleeping with Worth, however Bullard didn't seem to mind. Bullard had no right to claim any moral high ground as he was already married and had never bothered to divorce his wife. It was an amicable arrangement all round.

Worth, Bullard and Flynn didn't stay in England for long. They had money in their pockets from numerous robberies that Worth and Bullard had carried out in Liverpool, and in 1871 the trio left England and sailed for France. The Prussian army had recently besieged Paris, which was in a state of chaos. The city was an open book for someone like Worth.

Worth bought a bar at Number 2, Rue Scribe – a two-storey establishment. The first floor was a saloon and gentleman's club. It was a tastefully decorated front for the real enterprise on the second floor, an illegal gambling den. Apart from the money to be made through gambling, the bar quickly became something of a gathering point for American criminal expatriates. It was a good place to do business. Crimes were organised and specialists were recruited. Kitty Flynn was an immaculate hostess, Charley Bullard played the piano and Worth presided over the whole enterprise. Criminals, respectable citizens and business figures with a toe dipped in both worlds patronised the place. The most gifted and colourful thieves that were to make up the bulk of Worth's future criminal army were fixtures of the 'American Bar', as it soon came to be known. Worth made sure that he paid off key members of the Parisian police force to turn a blind eye to the bar's true nature. But in the unlikely event of a police raid, all Worth had to do was press a buzzer and his disciplined staff would quickly clear away anything incriminating. For three years the American Bar was at the criminal heart of things in Paris, but late in 1873 a stocky detective walked into the bar and shook hands with Adam Worth. The detective's name was William Pinkerton.

THE PINKERTONS

William Pinkerton was the son of Alan Pinkerton, a Glaswegian who had left his native Scotland for America, settling in Chicago. Alan's original profession was a barrel maker, but he developed something of a reputation as an amateur detective. In 1840 Alan's pastime became his profession when the Mayor of Chicago employed him as a police detective. A decade or so later he founded the Pinkerton National Detective Agency. Based out of Chicago, Pinkerton detectives could operate anywhere in the United States. They were not constrained by county or state borders and could pursue a criminal anywhere they pleased. They were highly trained, were experts in undercover work, were generally excellent at shadowing criminals and their intelligence network was sophisticated. Pinkertons were tough and independent men, comfortable with violence as a tool of their trade. They had a formidable reputation for tenacity and their motto was 'We Never Sleep'. Among the American criminal community, fear of the Pinkertons generally outranked that of the official agents of law enforcement. Famous Pinkerton scalps included the train robber Frank Reno and the Wild Bunch (Butch Cassidy and the Sundance Kid's gang, who the Pinkertons hounded out of the country). Famous Pinkertons would include the tracker Tom Horn and the crime writer Dashiell Hammett. Pinkerton life was naturally hazardous and there were inevitable casualties.

The Pinkerton National Detective Agency really came into its own during the American Civil War. Abraham Lincoln put great stock in their abilities, and they provided intelligence and personal protection during the years of civil conflict. But for an organisation that took so naturally to the art of 'state and corporate sponsored subterfuge', there was the inevitable dark side to their operations. Pinkerton detectives were often employed to disrupt picket lines in the violent Union disputes of the late nineteenth and early twentieth centuries. They could also be guilty of horrendous blunders. A botched raid on the home of Jesse James resulted in the death of James' 8-year-old half-brother and the maiming of his mother.

Generally, however, the Pinkertons' success rate was formidable. And while Adam Worth showed little fear of the various municipal and local police forces he would encounter throughout his career, he both feared and respected the Pinkertons. In fact, it was the Pinkertons that made the connection between the New York underworld and Worth's Boston robbery, and it was Pinkerton pressure that forced Worth to forsake America for Europe.

THE EYE

William Pinkerton was Alan's second son. William had an older brother named Robert. Both brothers held senior positions within their father's detective agency and would inherit the company when he died in 1884. Robert was the consummate administrator, whilst William was a field agent

William Pinkerton.
(Illustrated by Jean
Nightingale)

par excellence. William Pinkerton was a dogged manhunter whose seeming omniscience and tenacity earned him the nickname 'The Eye'. Like Worth, he had seen service in the Civil War. In the war's aftermath he had garnered a personal death threat from Jesse James, who swore he would kill William if he ever set foot in Missouri.

William Pinkerton's business in Paris was only tangentially related to Adam Worth. Pinkerton was pursuing other thieves and had tracked them to the American Bar. He was personally curious about the bar and Worth. He had supplied the French authorities with valuable information about precisely what types of people were operating under their noses. But there was something in him that wanted to push Worth a little and see with his own eyes this new emerging prince of the underworld.

The first meeting between Adam Worth and William Pinkerton was bizarre in its indirectness and civility. Both men knew exactly who the other was but neither would openly acknowledge the other's true identity. Pinkerton ordered a drink. Worth either bought or else offered to buy Pinkerton's second drink. Their conversation was affable. The subject of the conversation was 'the people that they both new'. The conversation ended with the two men shaking hands and Pinkerton leaving.

The amicability of the brief bar-room chat was followed by a succession of police raids that signalled the end of the American Bar's run of good fortune. Pinkerton was behind the raids. He harried and shamed the indifferent (and largely bought and paid for) police force into taking action against Worth's criminal Shangri La. Adam Worth, Piano Charley Bullard and Kitty Flynn narrowly avoided arrest. In the latter months of 1873, the three criminals left Paris and re-entered Great Britain.

WORTH'S BRITISH EMPIRE

In an indirect way Pinkerton had done Adam Worth a favour. As far as his ambition was concerned, Worth knew that the American Bar could only be a temporary stopgap. He was considering shutting down the bar anyway and moving to more fertile ground before William Pinkerton had paid him a visit. Pinkerton had simply accelerated the process.

Worth arrived in London wealthy from his Parisian and American adventures. He immediately began constructing parallel kingdoms and dual identities for himself. He bought a large house on Clapham Common called West Lodge. The house contained a bowling green, a tennis court and a shooting gallery. A lot of the more palatial furnishings from the American Bar found their way into West Lodge; it would be Worth's respectable residence. As

'Henry J. Raymond' he would successfully present himself as a well-dressed, cultured, pious, church-going London gent. He had even lost his American accent, replacing it with a credible English one. He would soon own a race-horse and a boat. Bullard and Flynn lived with him in West Lodge with their two new baby daughters.

Worth's second residence was an apartment at 198 Piccadilly. This was where Worth would administer his new criminal empire. The building blocks were already present. Worth recruited his soldiers and retainers from the exist-ing pool of mainly American expatriate thieves drifting around Europe. Many of his recruits were already known, tried and tested from the American Bar. Worth organised high-class robberies, subcontracting the work to gifted spe-cialists. He continued to make a point of generally not participating in the robberies he had organised. He went unseen by the majority of the people he employed and they seldom knew the identity of the man who paid them. Worth put up most of the money and naturally took the majority of the prof-its. But Worth employees were protected. If arrested, Worth would employ good lawyers. If convicted and imprisoned, Worth would bribe guards, or if that didn't work he would apply the same creative acumen to breaking his boys out as he would to robbing a bank.

He was still atypically ethical in his adherence to a non-violent crimi-nal code, but he was also a pragmatist. He lived and worked in a predatory environment, and others did not share his ethics. If Worth was reluctant to indulge in violence he made sure that he employed at least one criminal who had no such qualms. Jack 'Junka' Phillips was one of the few English criminals in Adam Worth's inner circle. He was a dim man. He didn't talk much and was not a particularly talented thief. What he was was monstrous in every conceivable definition of the term. Junka Phillips was 6ft 4in tall. He had a bristling ogre's moustache and had been a professional wrestler. He could pick up a metal safe and carry it on his back. He was a brutal and vicious thug. Worth dressed him in butler's clothing and more often than not, when out in public, Junka would accompany him. Junka's official position was as Adam Worth's manservant. But Junka Phillips was Worth's bodyguard; Worth's one nod towards the barely latent brutality of the world he lived in.

Adam Worth's main enemy on British soil was New Scotland Yard, in particular Detective Inspector John Shore. The detective inspector was no William Pinkerton. He was arrogant, boastful, a hypocrite and to Worth's mind, stupid and vindictive beyond the normal requirements of his profes-sion. Worth would feel obliged to deal with Shore soon enough, but for the time being Shore could wait. In the middle years of the 1870s Worth had a more pressing series of problems with which to contend.

FLIES & SPANNERS

The year 1875 was one of troughs and peaks for Adam Worth. Four members of his gang had been caught passing false letters of credit in Turkey. They had been tried and sentenced to seven years' hard labour. They would serve their sentence in a tough Constantinople prison. Inspector Shore had furnished the Turkish authorities with information and the Pinkertons were trying to have the gang extradited. Worth went to Turkey in person and managed to secure the release of three members of his gang through bribery. The man left behind in Constantinople was Joseph Chapman. Back in London, his wife Lydia was looking after the proceeds from the European adventure. She was harassed and assaulted by a Russian member of the gang named Sesiskovitch who wanted the money for himself. Lydia died as a consequence. It was an ugly affair and Sesiskovitch was ostracised by Worth. More trouble was to come.

The marriage of Piano Charley Bullard and Kitty Flynn ended. Piano Charley was now an incompetent drunk. His skills were degraded and he had become something of a professional liability, and he was still friends with the unreliable and treacherous Max Shinburn. Both Flynn and Bullard parted company and returned to America, Kitty taking their two daughters with her. Once free of Bullard, Kitty Flynn would marry into money and prosper for a short while as a socialite. Bullard would go from bad to worse and die in prison soon after leaving England. Both Worth's best friend and his lover were gone. Worth had a flesh and blood relative close at hand in the form of his brother John. But John was as much of a liability as Bullard had become. Worth's problems with his brother would oblige him to commit the crime with which he would become most associated.

JOHN WORTH & THE DUCHESS

Unlike Bullard, John Worth didn't have the luxury of blaming alcohol for his criminal uselessness. John was a naturally mediocre thief. Had he been anybody other than Adam Worth's brother, the crime lord would not have given him the time of day. Adam's sense of obligation when it came to his brother was a rare Achilles heel. He sent him on jobs that were far beyond his ability. In 1876 John was caught in Paris cashing a forged cheque. He was brought back to London and imprisoned in Newgate. He gave a false name to the police, but Inspector Shore knew exactly who he really was and sought to get at Adam through his imprisoned brother. Adam Worth needed to get John out of Newgate as quickly as possible, and spirit him out of the country and harm's way. The best way was to pay the astronomically high bail of

£3,500, then once John was free, smuggling him out of the country would be relatively easy. But Adam was being watched like a hawk by Shore and Scotland Yard. Any bail put up either by Adam, or anybody directly or indirectly involved with him, would be refused. Adam needed a third party to pay bail who had no discernable connection with him or his brother. In order to persuade such a person, Adam Worth needed leverage.

In mid-1876, London was in the thrall of art fever. Businessman and art lover William Agnew had just paid 10,000 guineas at auction for Thomas Gainsborough's portrait of the Duchess of Devonshire. The Georgian painting was a controversial work charged with eroticism. It had been missing for an age but had recently been unearthed and put on the market. Once Agnew had outbid his rivals, he sought to make a little money by displaying the painting in his private art gallery and charging the curious 1s for the privilege of looking at it.

The painting went on public display on 26 May at 39 Old Bond Street. Adam Worth and Junka Phillips were taking the air. They saw the crowd and bought a ticket. As Worth stared at the painting two things seemed to happen. First, he began to formulate a plan to get his brother out of trouble. He would steal the painting and blackmail Agnew into paying John's bail. Only after Agnew had secured John's release would Adam Worth release the painting

The Gainsborough portrait of the Duchess of Devonshire. (*Mysteries of Police & Crime*, Vol. III, Cassell and Company Ltd)

Old Bond Street, where the painting went on display.

back to him. But in conjunction with this thought process the seed of some-thing else was being planted in his heart and mind. Worth liked the painting. It got under his skin, and by all accounts it reminded him of Kitty. It certainly looked like the woman he had loved and whose absence he mourned. The two forces went to work, the pragmatic and the primal, one conscious and the other latent. Both impulses would exact their tribute.

The robbery took place around midnight. Adam Worth not only actively took part in the crime, but shouldered most of the risk. He brought two men with him, Little Joe Elliot and Junka Phillips. For such a grand robbery the plan was an extremely simple one. The three-man gang would position them-selves around the point where Bond Street and Piccadilly met. Elliot would hide himself in a doorway and act as a lookout. Junka's function was to lift Worth up to the gallery window. Worth would force entry and cut the picture out of its frame. He would paste the back of the picture for lubrication's sake so as not to damage the painting, roll it up and hide it beneath his coat. Once back on the street the gang would disperse.

The robbery went as planned. Worth took the Duchess back to his Piccadilly flat and hid it there.

In London the following day, when news of the theft broke, it became evident that Adam Worth, in terms of sheer gall, had eclipsed his previous best in Boston. But on a practical level the crime was a disaster. Through the machinations of a gifted lawyer, John Worth was released from prison on a technicality. The Duchess was now next to useless as far as Worth was concerned. Its purpose as a bargaining chip had been neutered and it was far too well known an item for any professional handler of stolen goods to go within spitting distance of it.

The presence of the Duchess created tensions within Worth's organisation. Elliot and Junka Phillips were fully aware of its value and wanted payment. Worth tried to placate them both with a mixture of lies and pay-offs, but neither man was convinced nor satisfied. Junka Phillips in particular was becoming a problem. The man Worth had initially hired to scare off rivals was becoming overly familiar and even threatening towards his paymaster. In truth, the relationship had soured to the point where Junka decided to betray Adam Worth to the police. Junka's treachery must have seemed like a godsend to Scotland Yard. He had arranged to meet Adam Worth for a drink in the Criterion Bar in Piccadilly. Two plain-clothes detectives were present, positioned at strategic vantage points around the bar where they would be able to listen in on the conversation between the two men. Junka would entrap Worth into incriminating himself regarding the theft of the Duchess. The police would arrest Worth and Junka would claim the reward that had been posted for information leading to the apprehension of the thief. It was a good plan, but for the fact that Junka was a transparent imbecile who Worth saw through in an instant.

Worth and Junka met as arranged, but Worth would not be drawn into saying anything self-incriminating. Rather than leave the bar, Worth allowed Junka to keep on asking leading questions. The less the scheme went to plan the more visibly angry Junka became, so much so that he threw a punch at Worth.

In the only documented act of physical violence in his long criminal career, Adam Worth laid waste to Junka Phillips. Giving away more than a foot in height, Worth knocked Junka to the ground, kicked him repeatedly in the head and then walked out of the bar.

The treacherous insider was now permanently exiled from Worth's circle. He had been dealt with in an unusually violent fashion for Adam Worth. The way in which Worth elected to deal with Inspector John Shore was more typical of the intricate retaliatory measures he usually took against his enemies.

Worth hated Shore. Shore had hounded and dogged Worth for much of his time in London. West Lodge was under a state of virtual siege. The Pinkertons had done something similar and for a longer period of time, but Worth didn't seem to hold it against them. He certainly retained an enormous amount of respect for William Pinkerton. Worth hated Shore because in Worth's opinion he was an incompetent idiot. Shore was a vulgar nuisance. The Pinkertons, in contrast, were good at what they did. Unfortunately for Shore, he had an

Adam Worth fights Jack 'Junka' Phillips and wins. (Illustrated by Stephen Dennis)

The Criterion Bar where Adam Worth brawled with his bodyguard Jack 'Junka' Phillips, and enjoyed a friendly conversation with his enemy William Pinkerton. (Mark Nightingale)

exploitable weakness: he liked prostitutes. He was a frequent visitor to the Rising Sun, a Fleet Street bar run by the madame, Nellie Coffey. Worth knew this and sought to engineer a police raid when Shore was visiting one of Coffey's girls. The raid failed to net Shore because of Worth's reliance on an old drunk he had hired and groomed to pretend to be a victim of theft. The drunk was supposed to complain that one of Nellie's girls had stolen from him. The timing of the complaint and the raid would coincide with Shore's presence amongst Coffey's whores. But the drunk, being a drunk, wandered off at a key moment and Shore was not present when the police arrived.

Little Joe Elliot, the third man involved in the Gainsborough theft, was less direct but just as treacherous as Junka Phillips. He had left England and was now operating in New York. He was arrested, convicted and sent to Sing Sing Gaol. Locked up and facing a term inside one of America's most feared penitentiaries, Elliot turned on his former employer and informed the Pinkertons that Adam Worth was the Gainsborough thief. The Pinkertons passed on the information to Scotland Yard and Inspector Shore. But if Worth had been unwise in his choice of compatriots when he carried out the crime, he had shown good judgement in making sure neither of them knew where the painting had been concealed. Without that crucial information there was little the Pinkertons or anybody else could do.

The truth was that wherever Worth was, the painting was never far away. He slept with it under his mattress. When abroad he wrapped it in his coat and hid it in a false-bottomed Saratoga trunk. And as Worth's empire consolidated itself, the increase in wealth and power was in direct proportion to the rapid departure from his life of old friends and confidants, as well as the treachery of once reliable compatriots. As he became personally more isolated, the painting became more significant to him. Worth was loath to part company with it. He developed a surreal and almost perverse sense of kinship and intimacy with the Duchess. In the latter part of his life it was virtually his most meaningful attachment.

THE HIGH WATERMARK

The 1880s saw Adam Worth at the apex of his power. His activities now extended beyond Europe and into Africa. He had an adventurous time of it posing as an ostrich feather salesman in South Africa as he tried to exploit the burgeoning diamond trade. After a failed attempt at highway robbery, that had him running for his life as a Boer guard attempted to gun him down with a repeating rifle, Worth resorted to a more signature methodology, leaving the country with $500,000 worth of booty.

Back in London, Worth proved that he was still one of the most creative thieves alive when he robbed Hatton Garden Post Office by cutting off the gas, inducing darkness and thereupon cleaning the place out to the tune of approximately £30,000.

Adam Worth then got married. The name of his wife has been lost to history but she was a respectable woman completely unsuited to criminal life. This was not a consideration as far as Adam Worth was concerned because his wife believed she had married a 'Harry Raymond'. They would produce two children together. When Adam Worth fell, his wife would find out who he really was, but until then it was highly unlikely that she was aware of her husband's true identity. Worth decided it was time to put the painting away. He travelled to New York and hid the Duchess in a warehouse.

In 1885, in the Criterion Bar, the arena where he had faced down the giant Junka Phillips and thumbed his nose at Scotland Yard's attempt to trap him, Adam Worth met William Pinkerton for the second time. By all accounts the meeting was coincidental. The tone was friendly. Worth still publicly maintained the pretence that he was Harry Raymond but the nature of the conversation was intimate. Worth praised Pinkerton to his face. He also cursed Inspector Shore, claiming that any advances Shore had made against him were only due to Pinkerton's assistance.

FALL

In October 1892 Worth was in Belgium. He had gone there to spring his old friend Piano Charley Bullard, who had been arrested and was rotting inside a foreign prison. Bullard died before Worth could execute any kind of escape plan. Although upset by the death of an old, if somewhat estranged, friend, Worth was still a pragmatist. He was in Belgium and decided to steal something while he was there. The target was an express van that delivered money from Liège station to various banks. The valuables were kept in a strong box in the van. Aboard the van was a driver and a delivery boy; the driver carried a gun. Worth had observed that whenever a personal package was delivered, the boy would do it. When a package had to be delivered near a bank, the guard would transport money to the bank and the boy would deliver the package, leaving the van, for a short period, abandoned and vulnerable. The trick was in knowing when the boy was going to deliver a package near a bank. These were easy conditions to manipulate. Worth personally arranged for a package to be delivered to an address near a bank. Meanwhile, Worth would be waiting nearby with two other criminals. When the van was abandoned, Worth would force the box open and loot the contents. The two thieves would act as lookouts.

Worth's associates were an American thief named Johnny Curtin and 'Dutch Alonzo' Henne, a local criminal. The crime took place on 5 October at 9.30 in the morning. As planned, the boy delivered Worth's package at the same time that the guard left the van; Worth then approached the abandoned vehicle. He located the strong box, broke into it and began to loot the contents. Two things went wrong. Worth stayed too long at the van and was spotted by a railway worker. This wouldn't have been so bad if the two lookouts had been doing their job properly. They weren't, and promptly vanished as soon as the commotion began to escalate. Moments later, Adam Worth was being chased down the street by police officers. He was quickly overtaken and arrested.

Adam was placed into custody, giving his name as Edouard Grav. During two days of intense questioning he said virtually nothing to the police. The authorities had little idea who their prisoner really was but rightly suspected he might be someone important in criminal circles. After five days they put out an international call for any information that might shine a light on the true nature of their reluctant guest. Worth's enemies began to come out of the woodwork.

Max Shinburn was serving time in the same Belgian prison where Piano Charley Bullard had died. When news trickled down to him that a man who sounded suspiciously like his old enemy was in Belgian custody, he saw the opportunity to feather his nest and revenge himself on Worth. Shinburn cut a deal with the authorities. He told the police who Worth really was. Furnished with an arsenal of incriminating detail gleaned from indiscreet conversations with the late Piano Charley, Shinburn laid Adam Worth bare. In return, Shinburn's sentence was reduced. Once it was clear that the prisoner was Adam Worth, more information flooded in. The New York Police Department verified that the man in Belgian police custody was the same man wanted for the Boylston bank robbery. Inspector Shore gave the Belgian police all the information he had on Worth, but there was one agency conspicuous by its silence.

The Pinkertons, who had been the most successful of all those that had pitted their resources against Worth, kept their own counsel and ignored the request for information. It was an executive decision on the part of William Pinkerton, who now ran the agency with his brother. William Pinkerton's motives for helping Worth were as personal as Shinburn's were for trying to destroy him. Although they had only met each other twice, Pinkerton and Worth had been in each other's orbit for most of their careers. There was an unusual affinity between them. They felt they knew each other and they certainly respected each other. The bottom line was that they liked one another and in their own mutually bizarre way had become friends. Although Pinkerton could not save Worth (nor would he have permitted himself to do so), he was equally unwilling to put the boot in along with all the rest. It was a gesture that would make no difference to the fate awaiting Adam Worth; but it was a gesture that Worth would not forget.

The trial took place over two days on 20 and 21 March 1893. Between his arrest and the trial the world had been made fully aware of Adam Worth's true nature and identity, yet he still maintained the fiction of his upper-class alias, Henry J. Raymond. He admitted only to the Belgian crime. Kitty Flynn briefly returned back into his life, funding his defence. But it was futile. Worth was found guilty and given seven years' hard labour. He would serve his term at the Prison de Louvain where Shinburn was seeing out the final year of his recently truncated sentence.

PRISON

Prison was the toughest period in Adam Worth's life. He was supposed to be in solitary confinement, but Shinburn reigned at the Prison de Louvain and solitary confinement did not stop Worth from being visited and beaten on a fairly systematic basis. Even when Shinburn was released, the abuse continued. Prison broke Adam Worth's health.

Worth's wife had been utterly humiliated by the news that the man she knew as Henry Raymond was in reality a high-ranking criminal. Worth had sent Johnny Curtin back to London to look after her. Curtin took it upon himself to sell everything that Worth owned at Lodge House. Then Curtin turned his attentions to Worth's wife. Curtin either seduced, or else doped and raped her. Either way, he took advantage of her vulnerability in a fashion that she would never recover from. Her mind snapped and she was institutionalised. Adam Worth's children were sent to America to live with their uncle, John Worth. On top of all this, news reached Worth that Kitty Flynn had died.

Despite appalling treatment, Worth's conduct in prison was good enough to secure an early release. In 1897 he walked out of prison. His empire was in ruins, his fortune stolen, his family scattered and his closest friends dead. He decided to go back to London.

OLD FRIENDS & UNFINISHED BUSINESS

Adam Worth's new London address was No. 66 Piccadilly. Although geographically very close, it was a far cry from the luxury apartment he had enjoyed at the peak of his reign. Worth still committed relatively ostentatious thefts. He funded a trip to America with the proceeds of a diamond robbery of Smith & Co., a merchants situated opposite where he lived. His haul netted him £4,000, a pittance in comparison with the enormous scores he had organised only a few years previously.

Whilst in America, Worth saw his children. He also paid a visit to a warehouse in New York and retrieved the portrait of the Duchess. Worth then travelled to Chicago, where he located the offices of the Pinkerton Detective Agency. He called William Pinkerton from a phone opposite the building and announced himself. Pinkerton invited Worth over for a chat. Worth walked into Pinkerton's offices, and their third meeting took place.

Their conversation lasted well into the night. Worth came the next day and the day after that. The two men were quickly locked in conference. The three-day summit between Adam Worth and William Pinkerton has to be one of the lengthiest, most bizarre and intriguing extended conversations in criminal history. There was a pragmatic reason for Worth's visit: he wanted to return the Gainsborough and he wanted Pinkerton to broker the exchange. His visit did not come completely out of the blue. Through cryptic letters, messages in newspapers and the efforts of a middleman named Patrick Sheedy, Worth had been testing the water for a while. But to walk into Pinkerton's office was unprecedented. For Pinkerton not to arrest Worth was unorthodox, bordering on unprofessional. Although there was business to discuss, there was something deeper that fuelled their meetings.

It didn't need three days to iron out the details of the painting's return. The meeting took that long because criminal and detective wanted it to. To

No. 66 Piccadilly Circus. As an ailing criminal Adam Worth still lived in Piccadilly, but in a cheaper apartment, in reduced circumstances. (Mark Nightingale)

some extent Adam Worth was a man coming to the end of his days, settling accounts the best way he knew how, with the only person on whom he could confer the properties the religious would grant a priest. William Pinkerton seemed happy to fulfil that roll. The three days concluded with Pinkerton consenting to work with Worth and see the painting back to London.

The two men would briefly meet one final time after this, but under more traditional circumstances.

The exchange of the Duchess took place at the Auditorium, a Chicago hotel. Present was C. Morland Agnew the son of Andrew Agnew, Agnew's wife and William Pinkerton. There was a knock at the hotel door and a man delivered a tubular item wrapped in brown paper. Agnew unwrapped the package; it was the Duchess.

The exchange was ostensibly mundane and lacked drama but for the fact that the man at the door was almost certainly Adam Worth.

A LAST ACT OF KINDNESS

Adam Worth's last address was No. 2 Park Village East, Camden. He had made some money from the exchange of the Duchess, much of which had been invested in bringing his children home to London. His son and daughter lived with him in relative poverty, still miraculously ignorant of his true identity.

Worth died on 8 January 1902. 'Chronic habits of intemperance' was given as the official cause of death. He was buried in plot 34288, an unmarked grave in Highgate Cemetery. But before Worth died he had written to William Pinkerton. He thanked the detective for his friendship and granted Pinkerton permission to speak freely about him once he had died, but with one caveat. Worth implored Pinkerton to be mindful of his children's feelings.

When news reached Pinkerton of Worth's death he went beyond what the master criminal had asked of him. Under the pretext of brokering an unpaid debt to Worth, Pinkerton gave Worth's son a cheque for $700. The son would eventually discover his father's true identity, but the bond that had existed between Pinkerton and Worth now extended in part to the son. Adam Worth's boy would eventually make his living working for his father's old friend and enemy: he would become a Pinkerton detective.

It took a little time for the death of Adam Worth to become common knowledge. William Pinkerton was obliged to publically say what he knew about him. A name could now be put to the extravagant crimes that had hypnotised Europe and America for decades. The public were fascinated by Worth's double existence. Shortly after Worth's death, Arthur Conan Doyle published *The Final Problem*, killing Sherlock Holmes and introducing his dualistic villain, Professor Moriarty.

THE RED-HEADED LEAGUE

Before Adam Worth's true nature became public knowledge, his previously anonymous crimes had influenced writers who had lifted his strategies and interwoven them into the fabric of their fiction. Arthur Conan Doyle was one of these, and the mechanics of Adam Worth's first great robbery wormed its way into Doyle's fiction. As one of the first Holmes short stories printed, *The Red-Headed League* is commonly believed to have been based on Worth's Boylston National Bank robbery.

In the story, Jabez Wilson, a pawnbroker, answers a bizarre advert in the newspaper to join the Red-Headed League. The league is a trust set up by the late Ezekiah Hopkins, a rich red-headed businessman. The trust has been established for the financial advancement of worthy red-headed gentlemen. If the applicant is successful, they inherit an eminently comfortable job. Between the hours of 10 a.m. and 2 p.m. the successful applicant sits in an office and copies out the *Encyclopaedia Britannica*. For his pains the applicant receives

£4 per week. The clause in the agreement is that if the applicant leaves the office during the prescribed time, then he forfeits the entire arrangement. Wilson applies, along with numerous other red-haired Londoners. After an arduous interview process Wilson is successful. He fulfils his part of the deal. As most of his business as a pawnbroker is conducted later in the day, the arrangement suits him down to the ground. In the early stages Wilson is monitored by a league member, but after a while the monitoring stops. Wilson turns up to the league office one morning to find a sign announcing that the league has been dissolved. He goes to Sherlock Holmes who resolves the strange matter in the space of a single day.

The league is an elaborate scam designed to get Wilson away from his pawnshop. The pawnshop is situated in the fairly reclusive Saxe-Coburg Square, but backs onto a bank on a main London street. Wilson has unwittingly employed a master thief as a shop assistant, and while Wilson is copying out the *Britannica*, his employee and another cohort are tunnelling through into the adjacent bank vault.

Holmes, Watson, a bank official and a police officer intercept the thieves in the bank vault. The main thief and architect of the crime is John Clay, a criminal of some reputation. Holmes provides a mini inventory of Clay's accomplishments. Clay is a 'murderer, thief, smasher, and forger'. He exists in two worlds. He is Eton and Oxford educated. His father is a duke. His public face is a respectable one. Holmes says: 'He'll crack a crib in Scotland one week, and be raising the money to build an orphanage in Cornwall the next.' Holmes admits to having 'had one or two little turns also with Mr John Clay', and that as a consequence he has 'one or two little scores of my own to settle', the implication being that Holmes has failed to net Clay until now. Holmes admits that Clay is 'one of the coolest and most daring criminals in London'. Clay for his part seems relatively philosophical about being caught by Holmes. Clay and Holmes enjoy a professional and courteous exchange in which Clay even compliments Holmes. Clay reserves his contempt for the police. 'I beg that you will not touch me with your filthy hands,' he says. 'You may not be aware that I have royal blood in my veins. Have the goodness also when you address me to say "Sir" and "please".'

The parallels between the robbery in *The Red-Headed League* and Worth's assault on the Boylston National Bank in Boston are pretty blatant. But Clay is an interesting mish-mash of Adam Worth and Max Shinburn, as well as providing something of a dummy run for Moriarty. Clay's double life and his genius for robbery are traits shared with Worth. Clay's affinity with Holmes reflects something of the bond between Worth and Pinkerton. Clay's arrogance and outrageous snobbery are all Shinburn. Clay's Worthian qualities are attributes transferrable to Moriarty. The fact that Clay had eluded Holmes on two previous occasions places him in the company of Moriarty as a rare opponent who bests (albeit temporarily) the Great Detective. All of this is all the more intriguing because Doyle, at that point, had no idea who Worth or Shinburn were.

WORTH & MORIARTY

By common assent, Adam Worth is taken to be Arthur Conan Doyle's principal inspiration for Professor Moriarty. Doyle's physical description of Moriarty bears no resemblance to Adam Worth, and Moriarty's background has no correlation with Worth's. Moriarty is comfortable with violence and murder in a way that was completely anathema to Worth. But the sophisticated, far-reaching and varied nature of Worth's criminal empire is reflected in Moriarty's organisation, as is his double life, and the degrees of separation between Worth and his army of thieves. The sense of kinship between enemies that links Holmes and Moriarty has its obvious parallel in the relationship between Worth and Pinkerton. As does the second-fiddle place of Inspector Shore in the Adam Worth story, reflecting Inspector Lestrade's inability to keep pace with Holmes and his best enemies. Worth had a larger-than-life henchman in the form of Junka Phillips. Moriarty had Colonel Moran.

Adam Worth was referred to as 'the Napoleon of the criminal world' by Sir Robert Anderson, a leading Scotland Yard detective. The quote reflects Doyle's famous description of Moriarty in *The Final Problem*. Whether Anderson said this before *The Final Problem* was published, and Doyle was alluding to Worth, or whether Anderson was quoting Doyle in order to describe Worth, is a contested point. The exact dating of Anderson's quote is difficult to pin down, but Anderson knew Doyle personally and was thought to have furnished the writer with information regarding Adam Worth. Conan Doyle also met William Pinkerton and they may well have talked about Worth.[1] However, for the most explicit link between Worth and Moriarty, a reader must go to Conan Doyle's last Sherlock Holmes novel, *The Valley of Fear*.

The Valley of Fear contains the famous description of Moriarty's office. In the office is an expensive painting of a woman with a lamb, *La Jeune Fille a l'Agneau* by Jean Baptiste Greuze. Neither the painting nor the artist exists. Worth biographer Ben Macintyre believes the painting is a cryptic joke alluding to Adam Worth's theft of the Gainsborough. The French title of the painting translates as 'The young woman from Agneau'. 'Agneau' is believed to be a variation or play on 'Agnew', the owner of the stolen Gainsborough. Macintyre is convinced that Conan Doyle used Worth as his basis for Moriarty and there is a powerful weight of circumstantial evidence to support the claim. But the evidence, albeit voluminous, is still circumstantial. As to who really provided the main inspiration for Professor Moriarty, the answer is in plain sight.

ADAM WORTH VS JONATHAN WILD

Doyle only references one criminal by way of explaining Moriarty; and that is Jonathan Wild. The Georgian gang boss has much more in common with Moriarty than Adam Worth. Wild possesses as much of the duality of Moriarty as Worth. Wild's power and position were dependent on maintaining a respectable front. His empire was administered in much the same way as Moriarty's. His criminal inner circle was colourful, dangerous and eccentric, just like Moriarty's. Wild had outlandish henchmen; but so did Adam Worth. Junka Phillips was a gigantic, ignorant thug, and although there is no evidence that Moriarty's Colonel Moran was explicitly based on anybody, Wild's inner circle of bodyguards, hatchet men and enforcers had more of the loyalty, intelligence, acumen and proficiency with firearms of a Tiger Moran than any of Worth's vassals. And although Worth was called the Napoleon of Crime, the Napoleon analogy had originated with William Harrison Ainsworth decades earlier, and had already been used to describe Jonathan Wild in the author's *Jack Sheppard* novel.

Worth's unique relationship with William Pinkerton has much of the symbiosis of the Holmes/Moriarty dynamic. There is no equivalent in Wild's career. But while Worth's great crime seemed to find its way into *The Valley of Fear*, and Worth's social veneer resembles Moriarty's more so than the more visibly decadent Wild, it is in the area of ruthlessness that Wild edges Worth out as the main contender for the Moriarty template.

The principles by which Wild enforced order and obedience among his own has its echo in Moriarty and his 'loyalty or death' ethic. Wild and Moriarty share a willingness to resort to murder for profit, self-preservation, revenge or expediency. Worth lacked Moriarty's ease with violence. Murder was anathema to him. Worth was too principled a criminal to be truly Moriarty. And while Moriarty respected Holmes and saw something of himself reflected in his enemy, there is no doubt that Holmes' murder, and Moriarty's execution, was the natural consequence of their strange bond. The Worth and Pinkerton dynamic crossed and re-crossed these ethical lines of demarcation in ways that Holmes and Moriarty would never have countenanced. But ultimately it was Adam Worth's unusual sensitivities regarding violence, and the depth of affection for the man who hunted him, that must relegate him to second place after Jonathan Wild as the ultimate Moriarty template.

7

FEASTING WITH PANTHERS

In the late 1800s, a young writer was walking through Teddington when he passed a large house and was beckoned towards the door by a woman. The woman was anxious. She told the writer that the house was being burgled; her husband was inside dealing with the intruder but needed help. The young man entered the house. He had a thick blackthorn walking stick with him that would serve as a weapon if the situation got out of hand.

Any image the writer may have had in his mind of a burly, heavily armed criminal was immediately contradicted by the pathetic specimen he encountered. The burglar was a skinny man. The writer would later describe him as 'a wizened half-starved creature'. The burglar was hiding beneath the kitchen floor, having gained access via a grate. He wouldn't come out and there was no other exit. The writer and the married couple kept guard and waited for the police to arrive. Nobody was in any real danger. The nearest thing to a weapon the burglar had was some builders' chips which he threw at the police officer when he arrived. The burglar was arrested, tried and sentenced to two months' imprisonment for his crime.

Up to that point, Bill Sikes was the epitome of violent working-class Victorian villainy and was the best-known burglar in fiction. His anonymous Teddington equivalent was more representative of the pathetic reality of nineteenth-century workaday crime. The Teddington burglar's arrest was about as far removed from Bill Sikes' spectacular downfall as it is possible to imagine. Yet the crime left its impression on the writer's mind. His response to the incident was to create a burglar that would challenge Sikes' supremacy in the imagination of the reading public. He would be the antithesis of both the Teddington thief and Bill Sikes. There would be nothing pathetic or incompetent about him. There would be nothing about him that was rough, crude or vulgar. He would come from the upper classes and members of the upper classes would be his principal victims. He would be the hero and not the villain of the story. The writer's name was E.W. Hornung, and his creation was A.J. Raffles.

HORNUNG'S BEGINNINGS

Ernest William Hornung was born in Middlesbrough on 7 June 1866. His father was German by way of Transylvania. He was an ironmaster who had moved to England in the 1840s, married an English woman and had eight children, of whom Hornung was the youngest.

Hornung was educated at Uppingham Public School, where his school years made an indelible mark on his imagination. His experience of public school was a positive one. He cut his teeth as a writer in the school magazine and, just as significantly, he discovered a passion that would prove to be a character in itself in the Raffles stories. Hornung loved cricket. Uppingham was famous for its elevation of the sport to almost sacramental status. Hornung was a disciple of the game and an enthusiastic and skilful player. Unfortunately, his health was at odds with his passion – he was asthmatic. For the most part he managed to play cricket while keeping his ill health at bay. But in 1883, when Hornung was 17 years old, his bad health won out. He was obliged to cut short his schooling and was sent to Australia to enjoy a more favourable climate.

The shock of leaving his beloved Uppingham was offset by the exotic new country in which he found himself. Hornung was to stay in Australia for two years. He worked as a private tutor in New South Wales to the children of the wealthy landowner Cecil Joseph Parsons. He became enchanted by the outlaw mythology of the bushranger. These frontier criminals were a dangerous and violent reality, but like their equivalent in the American West, a popular folklore had sprung up around them. It was this folklore, and Hornung's response to the more remote and savage elements of the Australian landscape, that provided another ingredient with which to flavour his crime fiction.

Hornung returned to England in February 1886 to tend to his sick father who was fatally ill and would be dead by the year's end. His family were living near Teddington and it was about this time that Hornung had his encounter with the burglar.

He was working in the city as a clerk but harboured strong ambitions to be a writer. He met with some initial success when a short story, *The Stroke of Five*, was published in *Belgravia* magazine. He wrote a novel that didn't do that well, but his second effort was taken up by *The Cornhill Magazine* and serialised. *A Bride from the Bush* drew on his experiences and observations in Australia. More stories were to follow and Hornung would use Australia as a recurring backdrop. He also began to explore many of the ideas that would find their natural home in his Raffles tales, including the notion of a gentleman criminal.

DOYLE

It didn't take long for the up-and-comer to attract friends in literary circles. Hornung would come to know figures as celebrated as J.M. Barrie and Rudyard Kipling; but the most famous and intimate literary friendship would be with the creator of Sherlock Holmes, Arthur Conan Doyle. The two men were members of the same clubs and shared a mutual love of cricket. The friendship was cemented by blood when Hornung fell in love with Doyle's sister Constance and married her.

Doyle's relationship with Hornung was generally affectionate and supportive, but occasionally characterised by streaks of ambivalence on Doyle's part. Doyle was initially quite taken with Hornung and financially supported him in the early days. He personally found Hornung to be sharp and witty. He even compared his wit to that of the celebrated Dr Johnson. But Doyle could also be quite condescending about him. Doyle believed in and encouraged Hornung's talent, yet wasn't averse to poaching the odd plot from him and using it himself. The two men would have a significant falling out over Doyle's friendship with Jean Elizabeth Leckie.

Doyle was in love with Leckie, but was already married. His wife suffered from tuberculosis. Doyle refused to sleep with Leckie while his wife was still alive. In Doyle's own mind there was no disloyalty. Hornung and Constance took the more Biblical stance that emotional infidelity was tantamount to virtual adultery. Doyle was deeply offended.[1] The two factions would reconcile in time. Doyle would eventually marry Leckie, and Hornung and Constance would accept the marriage, but whatever the sometimes choppy nature of their relationship was, Doyle was a significant element in encouraging Hornung to create his best-loved character.

THE IDES OF MARCH

In 1896 the Teddington burglary was transposed to Australia in the short story *After the Fact*. In it, the burglar is public-school educated. The victim (and narrator of the story) recognises the thief: they went to the same school (the narrator at one point having been the burglar's fag). Old school loyalties win out and the narrator lets the thief go, but the thief is shot dead making his escape.

Doyle really liked the story. He was particularly enamoured by the notion of an educated thief. He liked the idea so much he gently reproved Hornung for killing the thief off. He went as far as to say: 'A public school villain would be a new figure for a series. Why not revive him?' Hornung was not certain but Doyle continued to encourage him. Hornung's response was to refine the original idea and create a London-based anti-hero along similar lines to the dead protagonist in *After the Fact*. In 1898 *The Cornhill Magazine* published *The Ides of March*, the first Raffles story.

The story involves a young gentleman named Bunny who comes to visit a gambling associate at his Piccadilly apartment at the Albany. The two men have recently been playing cards. Bunny has been cleaned out and cannot pay his gambling debts. He has come to A.J. Raffles to tell him the truth, as the two men went to school together. Bunny used to fag for Raffles. Raffles is well known in London high society as a wealthy gentleman of leisure. A man who, according to Bunny, is 'rich enough to play cricket all the summer, and do nothing for the rest of the year'. Raffles does not seem particularly affronted by Bunny's confession and Bunny tries to leave. Raffles stops him. Bunny then produces a pistol and for honour's sake determines to kill himself, but Raffles calls his bluff. He waits until the pistol is at Bunny's temple, until it actually looks like Bunny will pull the trigger, and then he stops him. Raffles is impressed and agrees to help Bunny.

Bunny admits that he came to Raffles for help and intended to appeal to the loyalty of a shared public education for mercy. He also hoped to call in a marker for a past act of loyalty from their school days when Raffles was almost expelled and Bunny covered for him.

To Bunny's amazement Raffles admits that he too is broke and cannot help Bunny financially. Raffles asks him how far he would be prepared to go to get himself out of his predicament. Raffles hypothetically suggests crime as a possible solution. When Bunny agrees, Raffles elects to take Bunny on a short trip to see a friend who will solve their immediate financial problems. It is two o'clock in the morning and the two young men walk through a fog-encased London to a house in Bond Street. Raffles has a key; the house is empty. At this point Raffles admits that he has misled Bunny – there is no friend. They are above a jeweller's shop and Bunny realises that Raffles intends to burgle it. Bunny is offended but only because Raffles has lied to him. Raffles affords him the opportunity to walk away but Bunny refuses. Bunny stands as look-out while Raffles gains entry to the jeweller's via the empty house. The men walk back to the Albany, Raffles' pockets stuffed with jewels. He gives Bunny a stolen cigarette case as a keepsake.

On the way home Raffles explains that he had been planning the crime for some time. He had done all the necessary reconnaissance but realised that he needed a partner. It becomes evident that Raffles has done this many times before. He admits to having committed his first crime in Australia on a cricketing tour. He justifies his position to Bunny by saying: 'Why should I work when I can steal?' Bunny for his part is surprised by his own absence of guilt and Raffles expresses a desire to work with Bunny again. He gives Bunny another opportunity to walk away. Bunny refuses. The last spoken words in *The Ides of March* come from Bunny to Raffles: 'I'll lend you a hand as often as you like! What does it matter now? I've been in it once. I'll be in it again. I've gone to the devil anyhow. I can't go back, and wouldn't if I could. Nothing matters another rap! When you want me, I'm your man!'

The Ides of March is essentially a two-hander that establishes the fascinating and often perverse dynamic between Raffles and Bunny that will be the fundamental element in all the stories that follow. It is in essence a seduction story, and it is easy to read the relationship in homoerotic terms. Bunny narrates the story, and his descriptions of Raffles are highly sensualised. Raffles is 'handsome', possessed of a 'curling nostril … rigid jaw … and cold blue eye'. Raffles to Bunny is 'beyond comparison the most masterful man whom I have ever known; yet my acquiescence was due to more than the mere subjection of the weaker nature to the stronger'. Bunny's induction into a criminal lifestyle certainly reads like a seduction. Raffles never coerces. He always offers Bunny a way of escape yet subtly entices him at every turn.

Bunny's induction can also be seen in more metaphysical terms. Raffles is a distinctly satanic charmer, offering Bunny something in the way of a Faustian pact. Yet Raffles is also half-Faust, half-Mephistopheles. He has long ago made his own bargain with the devil, trading a life of risk-taking against the constant threat and inevitable consequence of disgrace, imprisonment or even death. He recruits Bunny for practical purposes but also because he wants a companion to share his secret life with. As Bunny reaps the material and emotional benefits of Raffles' activities, he also shares the prospect of his damnation.

Apart from the relationship between the two central protagonists, many other elements are present in the Raffles universe that Hornung would refine over the course of future stories. Raffles' apartment in the Albany doubles as his base for operations and is a virtual character unto itself. According to Bunny, Raffles' flat is 'charmingly furnished and arranged, with the right amount of negligence and the right amount of taste'. On his walls, Bunny finds 'reproductions of such works as "Love and Death" and "The Blessed Damozel", in dusty frames and different parallels'. The Albany is more often than not besieged by a thick and ominous London fog. It is also the gateway to Raffles' hunting ground, London's West End, and the moneyed houses and stately homes on its periphery.

THE AMATEUR CRACKSMAN

The Ides of March was a great success and led to a slew of Raffles stories. Each story built on the foundations set down in *The Ides of March*, fleshing out the relationship between Raffles and Bunny, and expanding Raffles' environment, methodology and worldview. In 1899 the stories were collated in *The Amateur Cracksman* ('cracksman' being Victorian slang for a burglar).

Most of the stories are centred geographically around London and London's high society. In *Nine Points of the Law*, Raffles meets with a crooked lawyer in the Cafe Royal to discuss the retrieval of a stolen painting. In the same story he meets the thief at the Metropole. In *Wilful Murder*, using a combination of trains, a hansom cab and shoe leather, Raffles tracks a receiver of stolen goods across London, passing through Blackfriars, High Street Kensington, Sloane Square, the King's Road, Clapham Junction and Richmond. In *A Costumed Piece*, Raffles' observations of a loud-mouthed nouveau riche thug at the Old Bohemian Club provoke Raffles to burgle him at his St John's Wood home. In *The Return Match*, the Albany itself is moved to centre stage as a police manhunt for an escaped burglar compromises Raffles, who has given the man sanctuary in his apartment. But Raffles occasionally ventures further afield. In *Gentlemen and Players*, Raffles uses his involvement in a Dorset cricket match as cover for an attempted burglary. In *Le Premier Pas*, Raffles relays to Bunny the specific details of his first ever crime, committed on Australian soil.

By the end of *The Amateur Cracksman*, the reader has a fairly comprehensive sense of the techniques and rituals Raffles employs when he is on a job. Raffles prepares scrupulously for each crime and is a strong believer in the art of reconnaissance. He is secretive to a fault. Even the presence of Bunny as a confidant doesn't change this. In many of the stories collated in *The Amateur Cracksman* much of the tension and black comedy is derived from Raffles keeping Bunny in the dark about key strategic elements in his plans, often placing Bunny in danger for the purposes of expediency. He insists on Bunny's absolute trust but doesn't always return the compliment, or justify the faith Bunny is obliged to place in him.[2] Raffles shuns all company and always sleeps immediately before a burglary. He also limits himself to a maximum of two drinks (always whisky and soda) before a heist. When out on the numerous jobs that fill the pages of *The Amateur Cracksman*, Raffles' techniques include painting the hands of his watch with luminous paint so that he can tell the time in the dark, placing Champagne corks on the points of railings so that he can climb a wall without impaling himself, and making friends with a guard dog in the days leading up to a burglary so that the dog will not attack him when he is robbing its owner's house.

Disguise is a key weapon in Raffles' criminal arsenal. Raffles is a master of disguise as well as a consummate mimic. His criminal survival is as dependent on anonymity within the London underworld as it is on maintaining a good reputation in high society. Blackmail is the biggest threat to him. Consequently, when he needs to fence stolen goods, he does it disguised as a Shoreditch thief. He maintains an artist's studio on the King's Road which he calls his 'private pavilion'; it is his alternative address should he need a hiding place, and a theatrical wardrobe where he keeps his costumes and disguises.

Some of the most entertaining elements of the stories that constitute *The Amateur Cracksman* are those moments when the reader is given access to Raffles' philosophy of crime and morality. As a consummate sportsman, Raffles is fond of cricket analogies and the stories are littered with them. But like everything about Raffles, his relationship with cricket is ambivalent. In the nineteenth century, cricketing social hierarchy made the distinction between 'gentlemen' and 'players'. A 'gentleman' in cricketing terms was someone who played purely for pleasure and sportsmanship. A 'player' played for wages and was considered somewhat vulgar for doing so. Raffles is a self-styled 'gentleman' in the world of cricket and crime. On a similar footing, Raffles sees himself as an 'amateur', in the Victorian sense of the word. Whereas today the word 'amateur' is indicative of incompetence, in the nineteenth century it denoted skill for skill's sake, free of the distasteful necessity of taking payment. 'Amateur' was socially preferable to 'professional', and an amateur's skill was seen as comparable, and in many cases superior, to that of a professional.

In the story *Gentlemen and Players*, Raffles commits a theft chiefly as an act of revenge against a cricket-loving aristocrat who has had the temerity to treat him like a 'professional'. But there is something disingenuous about Raffles' claim. Raffles has no income other than crime, so he is technically a professional. Raffles also isn't all that interested in cricket. Bunny observes when they first meet that despite Raffles' formidable public reputation as a sportsman, his Albany apartment is devoid of any cricketing paraphernalia. Raffles admits that crime has superseded cricket: 'What's the satisfaction of taking a man's wicket when you want his spoons?' Yet cricket affords Raffles something of an intellectual as well as a physical workout, and Raffles in his ongoing spirit of disingenuousness is occasionally caught enjoying the game.

Raffles' initial justification to Bunny for doing what he does is glib: 'Of course it's very wrong, but we can't all be moralists, and the distribution of wealth is very wrong to begin with.' Later on, when Bunny challenges the necessity of Raffles undertaking a particular job, Raffles' justification is markedly different and more honest:

> Necessity, my dear Bunny? Does the writer only write when the wolf is at the door? Does the painter paint for bread alone? Must you and I be DRIVEN to crime like Tom of Bow and Dick of Whitechapel? You pain me, my dear

chap; you needn't laugh, because you do. Art for art's sake is a vile catchword, but I confess it appeals to me … I would rob St. Paul's Cathedral if I could, but I could no more scoop a till when the shopwalker wasn't looking than I could bag the apples out of an old woman's basket … A man's reach must exceed his grasp, dear boy, or what the dickens is a heaven for?

As in the case of *Gentlemen and Players*, sometimes revenge is the motive. The lord and his family who have unwittingly insulted Raffles by socially downgrading him to the status of a 'professional', become victims simply because they 'deserve it and can afford it'.

'Out of Place at the Metropole'

The criminal universe that E.W. Hornung creates for Raffles seems superficially genteel compared to that inhabited by other fictional characters featured in this book. But it is, in its own way, just as predatory, requiring Raffles to have an opinion of self-preservation and violence. And like everything else Raffles says, his thoughts on violence are wildly ambiguous and cannot be taken completely at face value. Raffles' first pronouncement on violence is a pragmatic, qualified pacifism. On 'carrying a gun to work', Raffles comments: 'You mayn't believe it, Bunny, but I never carried a loaded one before. On the whole I think it gives one confidence. Yet it would be very awkward if anything went wrong; one might use it, and that's not the game at all.' On 'the intellectual appeal of murder', he says: 'I have often thought that the murderer who has just done the trick must have great sensations before things get too hot for him.' Bunny is naturally disturbed to hear this and Raffles tries to reassure him: 'Don't look so distressed, my dear chap. I've never had those sensations, and I don't suppose I ever shall.'

Naturally, Raffles contradicts any comfort he offers Bunny in subsequent stories. Raffles does carry a gun when it suits him, or else encourages Bunny to carry one. Both Raffles and Bunny occasionally chloroform their victims. When meeting one potentially dangerous criminal at a fashionable London hotel, the conflicting forces of social propriety and criminal self-preservation produce this response from Raffles: 'Revolvers would be out of place in the Metropole.' He elects to take a weighted cosh instead.

Raffles is at his most disturbing and revealing in the short story *Wilful Murder*. A moneylender who acts as Raffles' fence discovers his true identity and intends to blackmail him. Raffles makes the decision to kill him. He suggests his chosen course of action to Bunny, who is flabbergasted, calling the suggestion 'Rot!' Raffles responds:

A matter of opinion, my dear Bunny; I don't mean it for rot. I've told you before that the biggest man alive is the man who's committed a murder, and not yet been found out; at least he ought to be, but he so very seldom has the soul to appreciate himself. Just think of it! Think of coming in here and talking to the men, very likely about the murder itself; and knowing you've done it; and wondering how they'd look if THEY knew! Oh, it would be great, simply great!

Even the prospect of capture and execution holds its fascination for Raffles: 'But, besides all that, when you were caught there'd be a merciful and dramatic end of you. You'd fill the bill for a few weeks, and then snuff out with a flourish of extra-specials; you wouldn't rust with a vile repose for seven or fourteen years.' Raffles methodically plans his murder. Bunny objects but comes along anyway. Raffles never gets to commit his crime as another of the moneylender's victims gets there first and kills him. Raffles settles for getting the murderer out of the country.

In a way the story lacks the courage of its convictions, but it is a disturbing story nevertheless. Although Raffles never commits murder, the readers know that he is not only capable of the crime, but that it holds a powerful intellectual fascination for him. Murder is the natural extension of Raffles' pursuit of sensation. Theft has supplanted cricket. In time, murder could easily take its place.

In the final story in the collection, Raffles is eventually caught on a ship off the coast of the island of Elba. Bunny is also arrested. Raffles apologises to Bunny; he asks for his forgiveness and dives overboard. The authorities search the sea but do not find a body. Bunny is imprisoned and disgraced. On board the ship he thinks he sees 'a black speck bobbed amid the gray', swimming towards a nearby island. And in the ambiguous last line he observes: 'And night fell before I knew whether it was a human head or not.'

A FORM OF FLATTERY

The Raffles stories are witty and dramatic. London is economically but beautifully rendered. A sense of present tense London life sparks around the characters as they make reference to Gilbert and Sullivan, as well as contemporary criminals such as Jack the Ripper and Charles Peace. With each story, Hornung expands his world, introducing recurring characters that extend Raffles' reality beyond the page. With every new adventure a little bit more of Raffles' background is revealed. Hornung even indulges in a little playful postmodernist fun at the expense of the reader. In *Le Premier Pas*, Raffles takes over from Bunny as the story's narrator, relaying to Bunny the circumstances of his first burglary. The resolution is anticlimactic and Raffles admits this. He confesses to Bunny:

> The thing should have ended with an exciting chase, I know, but somehow it didn't … I'm sorry, Bunny; but if ever you write my memoirs, you won't have any difficulty in working up that chase. Play those dead gum-trees for all they're worth, and let the bullets fly like hail … Do it in the third person, and they won't know how it's going to end.

The modern perception of the Raffles stories, for many of those who have not read them, is of something more polite than the subtly subversive reality of Hornung's crime fiction. Raffles is, in modern terms, a charming sociopath whose anti-social impulses are generally held in check by an elastic and negotiable moral code. In *The Amateur Cracksman* he never does anything that repellent. His victims by and large 'deserve it', as he puts it. But as *Wilful Murder* demonstrates, the potential is there for darker behaviour, and it is this tension that makes Raffles a compelling and shrewdly perverse creation. In Raffles' duality, in his innate likeability, in the incredible taste he exhibits sartorially and artistically, in his sexual ambivalence, his loneliness, in the potential for greater darkness, Raffles is the great ancestor of Patricia Highsmith's homicidal forger Tom Ripley, Thomas Harris' erudite murderer Hannibal Lecter and Jeff Lindsay's principled serial killer Dexter Morgan.

In contemporary Victorian terms, the works that were most cited in reference to the Raffles stories were those of Hornung's brother-in-law, Arthur Conan Doyle. When *The Amateur Cracksman* was published in June 1898, Hornung dedicated the book to Doyle. The inscription read: 'To A.C.D. This Form of Flattery.' Doyle acknowledged the debt, saying: 'I think I may claim that this famous character Raffles was a kind of inversion of Sherlock Holmes.' It's hard not to agree. Like Raffles, Sherlock Holmes is the consummate 'amateur' Victorian. The Albany is a comparable headquarters to 221B Baker Street. The dynamic between Raffles and Bunny echoes that of Holmes and Watson. Watson narrates the Sherlock Holmes stories, while Bunny narrates the Raffles stories. Like Watson, Bunny provides the muscle in the instance of a physical confrontation. Holmes leaves Watson in the dark in terms of the bigger picture of his plans and strategies in much the same way Raffles does with Bunny. Watson is Holmes' intellectual inferior, as is Bunny to Raffles.

Nevertheless, while one of Watson's main narrative functions is to act as an occasional primer to Holmes' conscience, Bunny's role is more complicated. Bunny superficially performs the role of conscience to the mainly amoral Raffles. He raises objection after objection to Raffles' various schemes and stratagems, but always capitulates. When Bunny attempts legitimate employment as a journalist he cannot sustain interest once the prospect of a new crime resurfaces. Bunny is in awe of Raffles' 'evil grace', as he puts it, with a devotion that borders on homoeroticism. Ultimately in *The Amateur Cracksman*, Raffles destroys Bunny, denying him the spectacular suicide he reserves for himself, leaving Bunny to 'rust with a vile repose for seven or fourteen years'. Raffles is never demonstrative in his affection for Bunny beyond flippant displays. He never apologises, except at the end when they are both arrested. Raffles never expresses any embarrassment about anything he says or does, but he does register a brief and solitary moment of shame when he rebukes Bunny one too many times for failing to pre-empt his schemes.

There are other distinct differences between Holmes and Raffles. Holmes' version of 'professionals' are the blundering police officers of Scotland Yard. By contrast, the police in the Raffles stories are intelligent and implacable. Raffles fears the Scottish police officer Inspector Mackenzie, who surfaces and resurfaces throughout the pages of *The Amateur Cracksman*. And it is Mackenzie who catches Raffles, provoking his leap into the ocean. Raffles is more fallible than Holmes; he makes mistakes. His schemes don't always go to plan. He is sometimes bested by the police and other criminals, and many of his victories are pyrrhic ones. Holmes' world is more grotesque, heightened, diverse, colourful, gothic and violent, but the threat beneath the surface charm of Raffles' world is darker than much of Holmes'.

Doyle enjoyed the stories immensely. He said: 'I think there are few finer examples of short story writing in our language than these.' But in his typically give-and-take-away manner he expressed reservations about the moral tone of the stories, despite having encouraged them into being in the first place: 'I confess I think they are rather dangerous in their suggestion. I told him so before he put pen to paper, and the result has, I fear, bore me out. You must not make the criminal a hero.'

Doyle's reservations were unfounded. The Raffles stories that made up *The Amateur Cracksman* were published in *Cassel's Magazine* between February and November 1898. The collection was published in March 1899. The stories were an enormous success. Hornung was suddenly rich. He exploited the ambiguity of Raffles' apparent drowning and resurrected the thief, who returned to England with Bunny for further adventures. Between 1899 and 1909 Hornung wrote two more short story collections and a novel. Many of the stories followed chronologically from the end of *The Amateur Cracksman*; some of them were prequels. Raffles was eventually killed off. This time his death was definitive and heroic, fighting in the Boer War. There was even a successful stage adaptation. There was a smidgeon of the controversy Arthur Conan Doyle had feared when Christopher Smith, an American burglar, blamed the Raffles play for his induction into crime. Like Doyle, Hornung was forever associated with his most popular creation to the exclusion of almost everything else he wrote. But Hornung seemed more at ease with Raffles than Doyle ever was with Holmes. And whilst Raffles lags somewhat behind Sherlock Holmes in the frequency with which he is resurrected and reinvented, he surfaces regularly enough in television and movie adaptations, as well as literary re-imaginings, to ensure that Hornung's legacy is secure.

But one of crime fiction's great 'what ifs' was the idea of a collaboration between Arthur Conan Doyle and E.W. Hornung. Despite the sometimes spiky nature of their relationship, both writers seemed to fundamentally respect the other's talent. There were abortive attempts to work together, but the obvious collaboration, the collision of Sherlock Holmes and A.J. Raffles, never happened. The lost prospect of these two great Victorian amateurs, as either antagonists or allies, is a regrettable one.

GEORGE CECIL IVES

Certain details of Raffles' life and lifestyle were lifted straight from Hornung's childhood. Raffles was educated at Uppingham. His initials were the same as Hornung's housemaster. Hornung's great sporting passion became the skill that defined Raffles in legitimate society. But the main personality that formed at least the superficial skeleton of Raffles was George Cecil Ives.

Unlike almost all the other figures in this book who provided the inspiration for fictional villains, George Cecil Ives was not an outlaw in the traditional sense. He was a moralist and an activist. He did not seek to subvert the law. In fact, Ives believed in the rule of law but wished to radically reform certain aspects of it. Ives was a homosexual. He was gay in an era when the law exacted harsh penalties for sodomy. He was a supporting player in one of the great courtroom dramas of the late nineteenth century.

Ives was born in 1867, the illegitimate son of an aristocrat soldier. He was raised by his grandmother and educated at Magdalene College, Cambridge. He was a talented cricket player and had aspirations to be a writer. The notice he garnered as a cricketer attracted the attention of prominent authors interested in the sport, amongst them Arthur Conan Doyle and E.W. Hornung. Ives' sexuality was another patch of common ground that brought him into contact with writers, artists and poets that shared his orientation.

He was a spectacularly handsome man. He was intelligent and sincere; he could be depressive and often humourless. He was an activist and worked towards the cessation of the laws that outlawed homosexuality. Yet his relationship to sex was not straightforward, oscillating between enjoyment and guilt. Ives believed that the laws regarding sexuality needed to be changed, but was highly circumspect in terms of how he sought to effect that change. He believed in secrecy to an almost pathological degree. He was an obsessive diarist and his diaries were written in code. Ives' temperamental setting was to avoid overt confrontation.

His London address was the Albany – No. E4.[3] His apartment was festooned with literature, much of it of a subtly homoerotic nature. The capacious living space, coupled with its central West End location, became the gathering point for writers. The Authors' Club met at the Albany, and it was in this environment that E.W. Hornung encountered Ives. The Albany also had a more clandestine function. Many of London's gay artistic literary figures saw Ives' lodgings at the Albany as something of a refuge, a resource and base of operations for the more politically proactive among them. It was in this context that he met two charismatic, flamboyant and indiscreet figures: the great playwright, poet and novelist Oscar Wilde, and his lover Lord Alfred Douglas.

OSCAR WILDE & BOSIE

Ives met Wilde for the first time at an Authors' Club meeting on 30 June 1892. Wilde was attracted to Ives. Wilde said to him: 'What are you doing here among the bald and the bearded?' The initial nature of the attraction changed very quickly. Wilde would flippantly put the cooling of his ardour down to the moustache Ives was sporting at the time. But the two men had divergent philosophies of sexuality and were incompatible on many levels. Ives believed that homosexual love was imbued with an almost spiritual quality. He believed that the root of his personality was his sexuality. Wilde saw the elements that constitute any personality as essentially composite. A person was the sum of their parts determined by environment and experience. Their differences were manifest in their divergent approaches to their art. Wilde believed that the act of artistic creation was its own justification, 'Art for art's sake'. Ives believed that art ought to be the vehicle for important messages. Each struggled to comprehend the other. Wilde found Ives' didacticism vexing. He saw him as something of a homosexual puritan (his writing sometimes had the trappings of New Testament prose about it). Ives would say about Wilde, 'he is all art and all emotion'. He would say about himself: 'I am all purpose.' Yet the two men liked each other almost in spite of themselves.

Lord Alfred Douglas was a poet, the notorious son of the Marques of Queensberry, an aristocratic thug who prized traditional masculinity above all other virtues. Douglas' relationship with his father was dealt a blow that it never recovered from when the Marques was divorced for adultery. Douglas sided with his mother and nursed a lifelong (and reciprocated) contempt for his father. Douglas was handsome and charismatic. He had an implacable confidence that bordered on arrogance.

Lord Alfred Douglas, or 'Bosie' as he was known in more intimate circles, first met Oscar Wilde in 1891. They quickly became lovers. On many levels the two men were natural allies. They shared an almost identical libertine ideology, and they both had a need to publically test the borders of moral convention on a frequent and flagrant basis. As ambitious men they both benefited from their relationship in ways that would advance their respective careers. There was a mutual trade-off in terms of contacts with the gentry and contacts within the literary world. Yet there was an undoubted and passionate affection between the two.

Ives met Bosie Douglas in 1893. Ives was attracted to him; but Bosie was a polarising figure and it was hard to be neutral about him. Ives' relationship with Bosie was rendered complicated by the tension he felt between sexual attraction and a sense of incredulity at how the young lord pushed Wilde closer and closer to public scandal. Ives called Bosie 'the original Dorian Gray', and worried that despite any attraction he may himself have felt for the aristocrat, his predilection for chaos might damage the cause.

PURPOSE

The year that Ives met Bosie he founded a secret society. The Order of Chaeronea took its name from an ancient battle that took place in 338 BC, when Phillip of Macedon executed the 300 male lovers of his Theban enemies. Ives decided that 338 BC would be year one of his new 'faith'. The Order existed to provide moral, political and artistic support for the Victorian homosexual community. Membership of the Order came by way of a formal vow and an initiation ceremony. Membership was only possible if two Order members submitted recommendations.

In March 1894 Grant Allen wrote a broadside against homosexuality in a publication called *The Fortnightly*. Ives acted out of character and stuck his head above the parapet. He wrote an impassioned response that Oscar Wilde likened to setting off a bomb. Later on in the year, Ives and Bosie collaborated on a magazine. The title of the magazine was *Chameleon*. Its content included a poem by Bosie and a story by a young Oxford undergraduate named Jack Bloxan; the story was called *The Priest and the Acolyte*. It concerned a sexual encounter between a priest and a boy, and the subsequent murder and suicide as a consequence of their liaison. The publication caused a hostile reaction. The writer Jerome K. Jerome denounced the magazine and rallied for a police response. Ives wasn't happy with the magazine himself; he felt that Bloxan's story was seedy. There would not be a second issue. *Chameleon* did contribute one thing of lasting value, however. Bosie's poem, *The Two Loves*, introduced the now-famous description of the homosexual act as 'the love that dare not speak its name'.

In the name of the cause Ives made the Albany available for rather more arcane gatherings. He believed that homosexuality was an elevated mystical state and the act of sodomy had supernatural properties. Both Wilde and Bosie took solace in palmistry and clairvoyance, and Ives hosted a session with the thought-reader Campbell Dodgson.

CONFLICT

The Marques of Queensberry sought a reckoning with Wilde regarding his relationship with his son. In 1894 he confronted Wilde at his home. He also left a calling card at the Albermarle Club with the words 'posing as a sodomite' written on it. Wilde attempted to sue the marques for libel. He lost the case and put himself in a very dangerous legal position. In failing to refute the marques' accusations he had been officially exposed as a practising homosexual. Wilde was now liable for criminal prosecution for 'gross indecency, conspiracy to commit gross indecency and sodomy' under the Criminal Law Amendment Act. The marques relished the change in the wind and used his wealth and influence to trawl through the West End's gay underworld for incriminating evidence.

There were two criminal trials, both of which took place at the Old Bailey. Wilde achieved something of a partial victory in his first trial. His natural grace and wit as an orator won over many in the public gallery. The jury was split, obliging a second trial to take place, in which Wilde was found guilty. The judge made little secret of the fact that he hated homosexuals. He sentenced Wilde to two years' hard labour, the maximum punishment allowed for the offence. Wilde served his time at Reading Gaol. In transit to Reading, whilst waiting under guard on the platform at Clapham station, a man spat in his face. Despite a degree of kindness shown by the prison administration, even the modified regime of hard labour was too much for a body softened by comfortable living. Levels of sanitation at Reading were appalling and Wilde suffered from debilitating bouts of diarrhoea, his cell sometimes fouled with his own excrement. Wilde was torn to pieces financially: his plays were taken off the West End stage; an American tour was cancelled; an imminent production was cancelled; and any savings Wilde might have had were devoured by the Marques of Queensberry, who sued the playwright for £600 in legal costs.

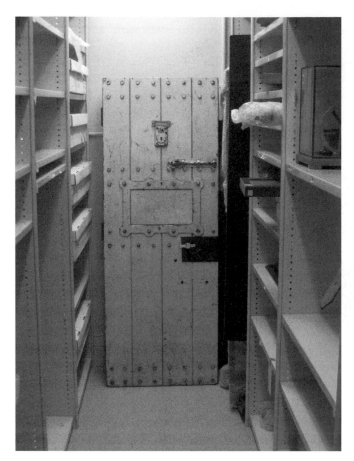

Oscar Wilde's
Reading Gaol
cell door. (Object
courtesy of The
Galleries of Justice,
Nottingham;
photographed by
Mark Nightingale)

In this time of crisis Wilde discovered exactly who his friends were. The majority fled. A few stayed loyal and offered support. Bosie, having pushed Wilde to sue in the first place, was in a semi-frenzy, tearing around London trying to raise bail. Wilde's friend Robert Sherard distinguished himself by trying to force the Marques of Queensberry into fighting a duel. George Cecil Ives played no direct role in Wilde's ordeals, but he was present and his function seemed to be to bear witness. Ives chronicled and preserved many of the thoughts, anxieties, observations and colourful details of the terrible episode. Wilde liked to frequent the West End's male brothels, and Ives called Wilde's rougher sexual assignations 'feasting with panthers'. Through Ives we are told that many young male prostitutes of the type that Wilde was fond, were corralled by the police and intimidated into giving evidence. Bosie wrote to Ives expressing his own sense of helplessness. Bosie and Ives both shared a desire for Wilde to curtail his own suffering by killing himself. Ives documented some of Wilde's prison conditions, including something of his routine and health problems. But when given the opportunity to make a public stand, Ives

The sculpture 'A Conversation with Oscar Wilde'. (Photographed by Mark Nightingale)

failed his friend. There was an invite from Robert Sherard to accompany him to Reading Gaol to see Wilde. Ives made excuses and didn't go.

To be fair to Ives, his personal feeling regarding Wilde's arrest was that the playwright had done the cause irreparable damage. However, Ives did seek out Wilde after he had been released from prison, when he was living in exile in France. Wilde was also reunited with Bosie. The last two years of Wilde's life produced two beautiful poetic works born out of his sufferings: *De Profundis* and *The Ballad of Reading Gaol*. But his health, fundamentally weakened by prison, was further dissipated by a lifestyle of heavy drinking and casual sex. Ives accompanied Wilde on a Parisian drinking binge. Ives remained sober, drinking warm milk, whilst Wilde grew progressively worse. Ives remained part of the circle of friends that visited Wilde until his death in 1900.

After Wilde's death, Ives became famous as a diarist and for his extensive collection of eccentric press clippings, but he carried on promoting the cause in his own oblique fashion. During Wilde's lifetime he had written two volumes of homoerotic poetry, *The Book of Chains* (1897) and *Eros' Throne* (1900). In 1914, in *A History of Penal Methods: Criminals, Witches, Lunatics*, under the umbrella of a book on penal reform, Ives included a case for the amendment of the law regarding homosexuality. The case for homosexual emancipation was foregrounded in a 1922 booklet entitled *The Continued Extension of the*

Criminal Law. In *The Greco-Roman View of Youth* (1922) Ives was more explicit in his advocating of the virtues of homosexual love, but from the safer, camouflaged vantage point of historical commentary. In time, Ives ratified his opinion of Wilde's public stand. He no longer felt so critical of his friend's open demonstration of defiance. He began to see Wilde more in terms of a martyr born ahead of his time and admired him for his courage. Although Wilde, had he lived, may have always been frustrated by Ives' reluctance to confront things directly, Ives was brave in his own fashion and earned his place in history amongst the early pioneers of gay rights.

As the model for Raffles, Ives seems to be merely the master thief's outer shell. Raffles looked like Ives. Raffles and Ives both played cricket to a very high standard. They both lived in the same apartment and they both shared double lives. But Raffles' personality bears no relation to that of George Cecil Ives. The sharp wit, terminal flippancy and flirtation with self-destruction is more reminiscent of Oscar Wilde than Ives. The ability to charm, tempt and beguile, and then lead the tempted to the brink of a precipice was all Bosie Douglas. Both Wilde and Douglas were sensualist like Raffles. Wilde drank whiskey and soda, exactly as Raffles did, whereas Ives drank warm milk. Raffles' philosophy of crime was 'Art for art's sake', Wilde's famous mantra. And although Hornung was believed to have based much of Bunny on himself, Raffles' sidekick seems just as reminiscent of Ives. Bunny's innate conservatism within an outlaw culture was more Ives than either Wilde or Bosie Douglas.

To what extent Hornung was aware of Ives' true sexuality is unknown. Hornung and Ives' literary circles certainly overlapped. Hornung may have guessed, and there certainly appears to be a homoerotic undercurrent to Bunny and Raffles' relationship. The parallels between Raffles' secret life and Ives' may be coincidence, but Ives was certainly the main inspiration for A.J. Raffles, and it is not outside the realms of possibility that Raffles was a composite of a trinity of personalities: George Cecil Ives, Lord Alfred Douglas and Oscar Wilde.

THE WICKEDEST MAN IN THE WORLD

M.R. JAMES

At Christmas in the early years of the twentieth century, in the warm and comfortable quarters of the provost's rooms of King's College, Cambridge, an eager crowd of educators and students waited to hear a ghost story. It was an annual tradition in the old university and utterly unmissable. The storyteller was a middle-aged academic with a talent for mimicry, who would read his handwritten manuscript to an audience keen for the festive winter cheer to be momentarily supplanted by a pleasurable sense of unease. The stories were in the main tales of academics (not dissimilar to the storyteller) who poked under the rocks of arcane and forbidden knowledge and unsettled something ancient and malevolent. The settings for the stories were invariably East Anglia. Cathedrals, bedrooms in boarding houses, deserted pathways, fields and clearings in the woods were the arenas in which half-glimpsed demons or ghosts settled their accounts with learned Englishmen. Before the stories reached their fantastical climaxes, the audience would have been teased with a subtle and gradual unveiling of the supernatural. The tales would begin with the mundane reality and routine of late Victorian/early Edwardian academic life. The supernatural would gradually intrude in the form of a noise, a sighting in the distance, a sense of discomfort or a tactile encounter immediately disturbing but easily dismissed by a rational mind. The stories would feel credible to the listeners and the creatures plausible because the storyteller would make reference here and there to a faux manuscript of his own devising, or a convincing piece of folklore he had made up.

The stories thrilled the listeners and acquired a reputation beyond their immediate intended function. Some of them were printed in periodicals and

many eventually collected and published in four volumes between 1904 and
1925. They are now counted amongst the best ghost stories ever written. The
author was Montague Rhodes James.

M.R. James was a paradoxical figure. He was an outstanding academic
who, in his long career, was both provost of King's College and Eton (where
he had been a pupil). He was an expert in the Apocrypha and was a pioneer
in the cataloguing of Cambridge's vast collection of medieval manuscripts.
His father was a clergyman who had wanted him to become a minister, but
James had resisted the gentle pressure to follow his father into the Church,
opting instead for the equally vocational (and quasi-monastic) existence of an
academic life. Although he rejected an ecclesiastical career, M.R. James was
still a devoutly religious man. He was warm and friendly, beloved by most of
the people who encountered him, yet his imagination was macabre. He was
a devoted fan of the horror writer Joseph Sheridan Le Fanu, but to James the
worlds of horror and religion were not mutually exclusive. His imaginative
life was liberated rather than repressed by the Bible and Christianity. As a child
he loved hearing of the deaths of Christian martyrs. He was particularly taken
with the apocalyptic passages at the close of the New Testament. He would
imagine the skies of East Anglia split by armies of fierce angels heralding the
return of Christ. The sense of the old and the strange – whether found in the
pages of the Bible, church history or folklore – never left him and are ever
present in his formidable collection of ghost stories.

The British Museum, a key building in both *Casting the Runes* and *The Devil Rides Out*.

In *More Ghost Stories of an Antiquary*, the second collection of M.R. James' supernatural tales, *Casting the Runes* is one of his best-known and influential stories. Although many of the classic Jamesian elements are present, *Casting the Runes* is an atypical addition to the James canon. Much of the action takes place in woods and abbeys and empty houses, but London also plays an important role in the narrative, in particular the British Museum. Another element that bucks the Jamesian formula is the emphasis on a flesh-and-blood villain, the black magician Karswell.

KARSWELL

Casting the Runes begins with its hero, the academic Edward Dunning, rejecting a badly written paper on alchemy. The author is Karswell, who is eager to discover the identity of the man who has dismissed his work. Dunning is made aware of Karswell's interest in him and seeks out information about Karswell from friends who live near him. He discovers that Karswell is wealthy and owns an abbey in Warwickshire; he is easily offended and vindictive to a fault. He is also the author of his own religion. Dunning's friends summarise everything they know about Karswell in one disturbing anecdote: he once invited the children of the surrounding area to attend a magic lantern show at his abbey. He began his performance with a version of Little Red Riding Hood, where the images and accompanying sound effects were more than a little realistic. Each slide became progressively more vivid and gruesome until the children were chased out of the abbey by images of snakes, insects and winged creatures that seemed to almost burst out of the picture. Dunning's friends' ultimate assessment of Karswell is that 'he has all the possibilities of a distinguished criminal'.

Dunning discovers that he is not the first to have offended Karswell in respect of his academic ambitions. John Harrington, another person who had previously savaged Karswell's work, was found dead in a wood with his neck broken. Dunning sees Harrington's name appear in the form of an advert on the car wall of a tram. The advert announces Harrington's death with the words: 'Three months were allowed'. The advert is not there the following day.

Dunning is studying in the Select Manuscript Room of the British Museum. He hears his name whispered and drops his papers on the floor. A man picks the papers up and returns them to him with the words, 'May I give you this?' Dunning enquires as to the identity of the man and is told that he is Karswell. From that point on, Dunning begins to experience rapid and increasingly intense supernatural visitations. He feels an odd disconnection with the people around him. His house empties as both of his servants

Edward Dunning is visited by a demon sent by the black magician, Karswell. (Illustrated by Stephen Dennis)

fall ill at the same time. The lights in his house fail. His bedroom door opens by itself, and the implicit becomes momentarily manifest when Dunning touches a mouth and teeth of something inhuman in his bed.

Dunning finds an ally in John Harrington's brother, Henry, who possesses some knowledge of the occult. He explains what is happening to Dunning and how to stop the magician. Dunning has been served a rune hidden in the papers that Karswell returned to him at the British Museum. The rune marks Dunning for death at the hands of a demon after a three-month period of torment. Dunning can do nothing to arrest the curse unless he can return the rune to Karswell without the magician realising.

The climax of *Casting the Runes* involves an elaborate game of cat and mouse between Dunning, Harrington and Karswell. Harrington spies on Karswell who has gone to ground. As time is on the verge of running out for Dunning, Harrington learns that Karswell is to take a train to the coast and leave the country. Harrington boards the same train at Victoria Station. Dunning dons a disguise and waits at Croydon West railway station to intercept the train. Dunning meets Karswell for a second time and returns the rune without the magician's knowledge. As Karswell leaves England, two men discuss whether or not they saw a dog accompany him up the gangplank and onto the boat. As the story ends, news leaks back to England that Karswell is dead, crushed to death by a stone mysteriously dislodged from the scaffolding of St Wulfram's church.

Casting the Runes is perhaps the best known of all M.R. James' short stories. It was adapted into the excellent 1957 film *Night of the Demon*. The central idea of a tainted artefact that will destroy the recipient if not passed on or returned is a recurring and adaptable staple in horror (Hideo Nakata's *The Ring* and Sam Raimi's more recent *Drag Me to Hell* are just two of many examples that owe more than a passing debt to *Casting the Runes*). But another reason why the story has continued to fascinate is because of its central antagonist and his perceived connection with a real-life occultist. It is widely assumed (and often reported as fact) that Karswell is a thinly disguised version of the infamous and iconic magician Aleister Crowley.

Like Professor Moriarty in *The Final Problem*, Karswell barely shows his face in *Casting the Runes*. He is limited to very few appearances: his marking of Dunning, the returning of the rune and his departure from England followed by the demon that will eventually kill him. Everything else Karswell says and does is reported second hand. Like Moriarty, we hear of his death but are not permitted to be present for it. Unlike Moriarty, Karswell's appearance is not described in any great detail. He is said to be 'stout' and have a 'rare face', but Karswell's bad character is in no doubt. Karswell's attributes are

Aleister Crowley. (Illustrated by Jean Nightingale)

distinctly Crowley-esque, as he was also 'easily offended', 'never forgave' and 'invented a religion of his own making'. If James only gives the reader two of Karswell's physical characteristics, then they are also applicable to Crowley, who was prone to obesity and indeed had a 'rare face' (if rare can be described as having a large bald head and penetrating eyes).

The problem with the above attributes is that they all fit the Crowley of the 1920s and '30s, the period where Crowley was at the height of his infamy. The precise dating of the writing of *Casting the Runes* is difficult to pin down. It was penned sometime between 1904 and 1911. At that time Crowley was a young man with something of a rising reputation as a troublemaker in occult circles. Crowley studied at Cambridge when M.R. James was still there; however, Crowley was at Trinity College while James was at King's. He was a controversial student but a fledgling in matters of the occult. Crowley was a member of the secret society The Hermetic Order of the Golden Dawn during the years straddling the nineteenth and twentieth centuries. His part in the power struggle within that organisation may have alerted James to his existence, but James made no mention of him in any of his surviving correspondence. Yet if the myth still persists that Karswell was based on Crowley, other writers good and bad would produce work rooted in authentic encounters with the magician. And of the numerous fictional works inspired by the example of Crowley, many would retain a crucial link to London.

CROWLEY

It is worth briefly comparing the early lives of Aleister Crowley and M.R. James. Both men were the products of highly religious families. Both were indelibly shaped by the English public school system. Although occupying contrasting moral poles, they were both essentially unreconstructed Victorians and both were drawn to the apocalyptic writings of the Book of Revelations. Unlike James, Crowley's interest in the Bible was less inspired by a sense of eschatological and literary awe and more by an over-identification with the Beast of Revelations. Where James embraced his father's religion, Crowley rejected it; and where James returned to his beloved Eton as provost, Crowley passed through numerous public schools and his relation with almost all of them was antagonistic. James' religion and family life nurtured and encouraged the qualities that earned him a formidable reputation as a scholar, a respected Christian gentleman and great writer of supernatural fiction. Crowley's early family life was repressive. His religion and education were brutal and censorious. Until at least his early twenties, almost everything Crowley did that was shocking and provocative was in some way a reaction against his family, his faith and formal education. And as much as Christianity recoils from a figure like Crowley (often with much justification), it was in part a fringe branch of Christianity that inadvertently created him.

Aleister Crowley was born Edward Alexander Crowley in 1875. He was named after his father who was a wealthy brewer and itinerate preacher. His mother Emily Crowley had come from poor beginnings in Somerset and was not particularly well educated. Crowley's parents were Exclusive Brethren, an extremely strict branch of an already austere denomination, the Plymouth Brethren. The Exclusive Brethren believed in the authority of Holy Scripture to the exclusion of all other authorities, including Parliament. They rejected church hierarchy and titles. Their doctrine placed great emphasis on the passages of the Bible that dealt with the return of Christ and his satanic inverse, the Antichrist. Non-Biblical reading was either forbidden, vetted or frowned upon.

Little of the above bothered Aleister Crowley overly while his father was alive. Crowley hero-worshipped his father and would accompany him on preaching journeys. His relationship with his mother was always strained, but any contempt he felt for her was held in check while his father lived. Edward Crowley senior contracted cancer of the tongue. His wealth meant that he could afford the best doctors available but the Exclusive Brethren steered him towards electro-homoeopathy, an alternative remedy that would prove ineffective. Edward Crowley died in 1886; his son was devastated. The loss marked Crowley permanently and either birthed, or else unlocked, a rebellion in him exacerbated and provoked by his mother's attempts to control and school him in a manner consistent with a good Brethren child. For his part, Crowley blamed the Brethren for his father's death and would quickly grow to hate Christianity with a passion (although he did retain something of a respect for the person of Christ).

Even while his father was alive Crowley had a difficult time at school. He was overweight and looked odd; he was bullied. After his father's death his mother moved to Thistle Grove in London. She looked to her brother, Tom Bishop, to help her raise and educate her son. Bishop placed Crowley in a school in Cambridge with a Brethren headmaster and here he was badly treated. An accusation was made that he had corrupted a boy, and his schoolmates ritualistically shunned him. The accusation was almost certainly groundless and Tom Bishop, to his credit, removed Crowley from the school.

It was during this time that Crowley conducted a disturbing experiment. He wondered whether he was capable of committing an act of cruelty that violated his conscience, purely as an exercise in willpower. The victim of the experiment was a cat, which he killed just to prove that he could. The act distressed him but he went through with it regardless, the mastering of his own distaste and revulsion being the point of the experiment.

On his return to London, Crowley was sent to a day school in Streatham. He constructed a rocket which he intended to set off on 5 November in the school playground. The rocket blew up and did damage to the school building. The explosion could easily have killed people but nobody was hurt, with the exception of Crowley who almost permanently blinded himself.

Crowley's education in the chaotic years prior to university was a succession of schools and private tutors. He was making the transition from victim to aggressor as he began to assert himself. He wanted greater freedom of reading material. Under his mother's scrutiny books were vetted, the criteria for an inappropriate book often absurd. Along with forbidden texts like *The Ancient Mariner* or anything by Emil Zola, *David Copperfield* was banned because a mischievous character in the book shared the same first name as Crowley's mother. Crowley took solace in *Paradise Lost* and found a hero he could admire in the form of the poet John Milton's interpretation of Satan.

Crowley's relationship with his tutors and schoolmasters was testy to say the least (at one point deteriorating into a fistfight), but his education yielded two things he would be grateful for. Archibald Douglas was Crowley's first mentor. He was a tutorial wolf in sheep's clothing who, although initially approved of by Emily Crowley, inducted her son into a world of smoking, billiards and sex during a trip to Torquay. As a tutor, Douglas didn't last very long. It is unlikely that Crowley was a virgin when he went to Torquay, but on his return sex became Crowley's great pursuit. Shortly after Torquay, Crowley was expelled from school when he contracted syphilis, the result of an encounter with a prostitute.

The other skill Crowley mastered during this period was rock climbing. He had his first taste of the sport during a trip to Skye with his mother. During the complicated ping-pong of schools and tutors, Crowley found himself in Eastbourne where he was obliged to live under the supervision of a teacher. His one consolation was Beachy Head and its chalk rock face. He was not a naturally strong person, but on Beachy Head he developed and practised innovative techniques of continuous motion climbing that mitigated his lack of strength. Crowley would go on to become one of the great (if rather unsung) mountaineers of the early twentieth century.

CAMBRIDGE

In 1885 Crowley entered Trinity College, Cambridge. He was 20 years old. He was finally free of the constraints of family and the Exclusive Brethren. He now changed his name from Edward to Aleister. His initial professional ambitions were to join the Civil Service, but they were rapidly superseded by the twin desire to subsume himself in the great writing previously denied him and further indulge his sexual appetites. He devoured literature, his favourite poet being Shelley. He idolised the explorer, translator and sexologist Sir Richard Francis Burton. He wanted to be a great poet. He worked his way through a series of town girls and prostitutes and caught another venereal disease. His only emotional sexual attachment was with Herbert Charles Pollitt, a female impersonator.

It was at Trinity that Aleister Crowley's interest in ritual magic really took root. One New Year's Eve, Crowley experienced something of an epiphany; he became aware within himself of a powerful potential for magic. He dismissed forever the notion of a conventional career path and determined to spend the rest of his life in the pursuit and mastery of hidden knowledge. Finances were no longer any kind of impediment to Crowley's pilgrimage – he was extremely rich due to an immense fortune he had inherited on his 21st birthday. He read numerous books and translations of occult lore and practice. The key text for Crowley was *The Cloud Upon the Sanctuary* by Karl von Eckartshausen. The formative idea that Crowley took from Eckartshausen was the notion of an elite society of favoured individuals who were the custodians of secret knowledge. Crowley left Trinity in May 1898. He didn't receive his degree and didn't much care. University had served its purpose in introducing him to the writings of Eckartshausen, and Aleister Crowley determined to discover Eckartshausen's secret society for himself.

THE HERMETIC ORDER OF THE GOLDEN DAWN

Whilst on holiday in the Alps, Crowley met a kindred spirit in Julian Baker. Baker was a chemist by profession but attracted Crowley's interest due to his knowledge of alchemy. The two men talked and it was obvious after a while that Baker's knowledge far exceeded Crowley's and extended beyond a simple academic interest. Crowley opened his heart to Baker, eventually revealing his desire to discover the secret society spoken of by Eckartshausen. Baker was sympathetic and arranged a meeting with George Cecil Jones, a fellow chemist and student of magic. Jones schooled Crowley in the rudiments of magical practice and introduced him to further vital occult texts. Through these two men Crowley was made aware of the existence of The Hermetic Order of the Golden Dawn, of which Baker and Jones were both members.

The Order's origins were complicated, its doctrines even more so. Its roots lay in the writings of the medium Helena Petrovna Blavatsky who believed in the existence of supernatural creatures called Mahatmas. These creatures (that also went by the names Hidden Masters or Secret Chiefs) were thought to live in the Himalayan Mountains. Their purpose was to monitor and steer human history. Access to their knowledge was permitted to a select and disciplined few who had mastered various rites and rituals. Members of the Golden Dawn were drawn from the cream of Victorian society and included the actress Florence Far Emery, the tea heiress Annie Horniman, the historian A.E. White and the poet W.B. Yeats. The Golden Dawn's leader was the charismatic Samuel Liddell Mathers, who claimed to have personally encountered the Secret Chiefs. Crowley had read Mathers' work *The Kabbalah Revealed* and had been greatly affected by it. He was convinced that he had found Eckartshausen's secret society.

Jones and Baker had little trouble persuading the Order to induct Crowley into its ranks. His initiation took place in London in November 1898. The exact location isn't known but in all probability it happened in Mark Mason's Hall near Southwark Bridge. Crowley would have been robed and hooded during the ceremony. Asked the reason for joining he would have given a formal response. He would have sworn an oath vowing never to reveal the secrets of the Order; the consequences of breaking the oath were death or paralysis. He was given a new name, Pedurabo, which meant He Who Will Endure.

An Order member's rank was measured by attaining degrees. Mastery of certain rituals coupled with theoretical knowledge would earn the Order member a degree. Crowley's rise through the ranks of the Order was initially swift, but after a year he found that he was permitted to advance no further. The reasons for the Order's obstruction of Crowley are not crystal clear, but probably had something to do with his unconventional sexual practices. Also, The Hermetic Order was essentially benign in intent. Crowley saw white and black magic as equally useful to him, a point of view that posed a probable threat to the integrity of the Order.

In the middle of all of this, Crowley bought a large house in Scotland near Loch Ness. The house was called Bolskein. Crowley was believed to have conducted many magical experiments within the walls of Bolskein, of the type unlikely to be approved of by the majority of the Golden Dawn. Before long the house had a reputation among the locals as a place where strange and bad things happened. The most fanciful tale involved workers fleeing from the house on account of an army of demons dancing inside it. The locals tended to give Bolskein a wide berth.

The speed, in private, with which Crowley was advancing in ritual magic was not being replicated within the Order. Crowley was frustrated and resentful. His situation coincided with a rift amongst the leadership of the Order. Samuel Liddell Mathers was living in Paris and directing Order affairs from there. His style of leadership was totalitarian. He claimed a virtual monopoly on access to the Secret Chiefs and demanded absolute obedience from Order members. Tensions had developed between Mathers and his London representative Florence Far Emery. Many of the London members had begun to have misgivings about certain doctrinal and financial matters. The London consensus was that Mathers had gone mad. Mathers' response was to accuse Emery of slander and divisive behaviour, and then dismiss her from the Order. Crowley threw in his lot with Mathers. He went to Paris and declared his allegiance. The battle lines were drawn and Crowley was sent back to London to seize control of the temple of the Golden Dawn.

The location of the temple was 36 Blythe Road. Crowley entered the temple but was ejected. As a first blow against an insubordinate membership by Mathers' newly appointed representative, it was a disappointingly temporal affair. There would have been many members of the Order who expected the matter to be settled by way of a magical duel and feared the consequences. When Crowley arrived at Blythe Road the following day he certainly looked like something that might have been summoned from a mystical plane. He wore a black mask, a gold cross and was armed with a dagger; W.B. Yeats confronted him. The matter was messily resolved either by physical force or by the intervention of the police and the threat of legal action. Crowley was forced to return to Paris and both he and Mathers were kicked out of the Order.

HIMALAYAN INTERLUDE

In 1900, shortly after the humiliation of the Golden Dawn episode, Crowley went abroad for a while. He travelled through the United States down to Mexico, where he claimed to have mastered the art of invisibility. He met up with his friend, the mountaineer Oscar Eckenstein, and they climbed Iztaccihuatl and Popocatepetl. Crowley travelled from Mexico to Ceylon and met Alan Bennett, a friend from his university years. Bennett was a devoted Buddhist and disciplined yoga practitioner. Crowley studied yoga under Bennett before travelling to India to meet up with Eckenstein again. The two men were part of an expedition that attempted to climb K2. It was an historic, courageous and perilous attempt that left Crowley snow blind for a while. Crowley went to Egypt and then returned to France, where he met the first writer to contribute a significant, authenticated portrait of him.

MAUGHAM & CROWLEY

William Somerset Maugham came to a career in writing by way of a double bereavement, an unorthodox education and a brief career in medicine. He was born in France in 1874. Both of his parents died when he was a child. He was sent to England and raised by his uncle, and suffered a boarding school education in Canterbury. It was a severe regime to which he did not respond particularly well, developing a stammer that never left him. He left school at 16 to study philosophy and literature at Heidelberg University. He then returned to England to study medicine at St Thomas' Hospital. His period of training lasted five years during which time he worked as an obstetric clerk in London in the slums of Lambeth. His experience as a clerk formed the basis of his first novel, *Liza of Lambeth*. The novel was successful and purchased the freedom to give up medicine and write full time. Six years of relative success followed, with Maugham's output alternating between novels and plays. In those six years he failed to duplicate the popularity of his first book, but was nevertheless managing to sustain himself financially. Although not wealthy, he was a fashionable presence at parties and by his own admission was having fun. But he was also conscious of the fact that he had reached a creative plateau and needed to do something radical if he were to advance artistically. Maugham made the decision to leave England and relocate to Paris. He rented a fifth-floor two-bedroom apartment amongst the predominantly expatriate community of artists who congregated around the city's Left Bank. A favourite meeting place was the upper rooms of Le Chat Blanc, a restaurant on the rue d'Odessa, where artists of various disciplines met to drink, eat and debate. Maugham very quickly became part of this scene and it was in this context that the writer met Aleister Crowley.

Crowley had been introduced to the community at Le Chat Blank by the painter Gerald Kelley. Maugham's initial reaction to Crowley was suppressed hostility. The Crowley that Maugham encountered was a physically large man who dressed every bit the part of the libertine occultist. He was opinionated, immoral, a gossip and a braggart who made bold claims for himself as an expert in magical practices. Maugham would never shake the initial contempt he felt for the man, but his dislike was balanced by an overpowering fascination. However, just when Maugham had Crowley pegged as a profoundly gifted flannel artist, he discovered that some of the magician's more preposterous boasts were actually true. Maugham had to concede a degree of respect for Crowley when his stories of having climbed K2 were authenticated. Maugham was also taken with Crowley's eyes and his powerful and unnerving stare. He was aware of Crowley's continued experiments in ritual magic (which the writer erroneously interpreted as Satanism). He dismissed Crowley's practice as an affectation motivated more by the Parisian trend for all things occult than any real sense of pilgrimage.

Maugham and Crowley were in and out of each other's company. Despite Maugham's ongoing antipathy, exposure to such a colourful and polarising figure was too good an opportunity not to exploit. In 1906 Maugham began work on *The Magician* and Aleister Crowley became Oliver Haddo.

THE MAGICIAN

The plot of *The Magician* is fairly simple. Arthur Burdon is an English surgeon of some prominence who has visited Paris to observe French surgical techniques. Present with him are his fiancée, Margaret, and her best friend Susie. Their guide around Paris is fellow surgeon called Dr Porhoet, an amateur scholar who has an academic interest in the occult. At a meeting of artists, in the upper room of a popular restaurant, they encounter the self-confessed magician Oliver Haddo, whose interest in the occult is anything but academic. Almost in spite of themselves the friends become part of Haddo's social circle.

Arthur and Margaret dislike Haddo, but Susie is fascinated by him. Dr Porhoet is polite but retains a respectful detachment. Haddo's constant presence, his contentious personality and his increasingly bold claims, begin to play on Arthur and Margaret's nerves.

Animals react violently to Haddo whenever he is near them. A dog bites him and he kicks it. Arthur loses his temper and physically attacks Haddo.

Oliver Haddo. (Illustrated by Jean Nightingale)

Haddo is humiliated but feigns remorse and begs Arthur and his companion's forgiveness. Haddo bides his time and exacts his revenge, employing magic to steal Margaret away from Arthur. He appears in her dreams and she begins to feel an inexplicable attraction towards him. He tricks Margaret into being alone with him and puts her into a trance. She has a vision of hell; she meets Haddo in the vision and is seduced by him. When she is brought out of the vision her will is broken and she becomes Haddo's puppet. Margaret breaks off her engagement to Arthur and marries Haddo. Much of the rest of the plot of *The Magician* oscillates between Paris and London, as Arthur, Susie and Dr Porhoet try to wrest Margaret from Haddo's control.

As the story progresses, Haddo's revenge reveals a more strategic dimension. His ultimate goal is to challenge the supremacy of God by creating life. He is obsessed with an old text that contains a formula for creating a demonic life form called homunculi. The key ingredient to performing the rite is a virgin's blood. Margaret is a virgin when she marries Haddo and although he degrades her at every turn, he never sleeps with her, electing instead to siphon her blood, bit by bit, as he conducts his experiment. The friends fail to save Margaret and she dies of a heart attack, her system weakened through loss of blood. Arthur vows to destroy Haddo but the surviving three friends are bested by him at every turn. It is only when Arthur abandons his scepticism regarding the supernatural, and Dr Porhoet is persuaded to apply his knowledge of the occult, that Haddo is defeated. Although magic plays its part in undermining Haddo, he is eventually killed in a hand-to-hand fight with Arthur. With Haddo dead the full extent of his experiments are revealed in the form of row upon row of half-formed homunculi, the last of which almost resembles Haddo himself.

The Magician is a double-minded work. Tension is subtly built in opening chapters until the narrative stops for a long digressive anecdote, or a lecture on some point of occult history or lore. The second half has a repetitious quality as characters pivot endlessly between France and England. Paris and London are nicely contrasted. Paris is a city of malevolent funfairs, arcane book collections, art galleries, fashionable restaurants and Catholic seminaries. It is a place where impossible things might happen. The London of *The Magician* is a city of pristine hotels and opera houses. Many of the novel's supernatural encounters happen in Paris. When Haddo is confronted in London, he uses the law to exert leverage over his enemies rather than magic. London only becomes sinister when it is the backdrop to an anecdote about Haddo's past – visiting opium dens in the East End – and features in a story told by Haddo of a Frenchman who calls up the ghost of Appolonius of Tyrone. The final series of supernatural confrontations takes place in England, but in and around Haddo's large Staffordshire house, 'Skein'.

The Magician is at its best whenever Maugham describes something supernatural. Margaret's vision of hell is intense and hallucinogenic, climaxing in an unforgettable succession of images as a tree split by lightning becomes a mess of human arms and legs and then transforms into the pagan deity Pan.

Maugham's heroes are weakly written, their stock character traits pedantically over-explained. Oliver Haddo is a different matter. He animates and usurps every scene he appears in. If in M.R. James a little Crowley goes a long way, Maugham is of the opposite opinion, allowing his readers to gorge themselves on Haddo in all his obese glory.

HADDO

Oliver Haddo was, by Maugham's own admission, an exaggerated and far more malicious version of the real thing, but there is much of Crowley in *The Magician*. Although only 27, on the verge of complete baldness and overweight when Maugham knew him, a pretty accurate facsimile of what Crowley would look like in a few years' time was created by Maugham. Haddo's evil nature is defined physically by his girth, and during the book he actually becomes fatter and fatter the more his true nature becomes apparent. At the novel's close Haddo is almost a parody of obesity. The stare that fascinated Maugham so much is put to good use in the novel. Crowley's ability to tell an apparently tall story that turns out to be true finds its equivalent in Haddo's lengthy hunting anecdote, in which he claims to have killed three African lions with three consecutive shots. Haddo, like Crowley, is a well-travelled mountaineer. His Staffordshire house and estate is Bolskein transposed to the West Midlands, complete with Bolskein's reputation for supernatural phenomena. When Haddo enchants Margaret he quotes Crowley's old adversary W.B. Yeats. Haddo's grand entrance is the disruptive gatecrashing of a meeting of artists, not dissimilar to that which took place above Le Chat Blanc. The numerous passages in *The Magician* where occult lore is spouted have more than a ring of authenticity about them. In fact, Maugham borrowed many occult texts from his friend Gerald Kelley. Many of the books Kelley loaned to Maugham were recommended to him by Crowley.

The Magician was published in 1909. It was originally meant to be part of a three-book deal with the publisher Methuen, but Methuen was horrified by it and returned the novel to Maugham. It was subsequently bought and published by William Heinemann. *The Magician* divided critics into those who were revolted by its extremities and those who appreciated its virtues as a thrilling and experimental work of supernatural fiction. Crowley was ambivalent about it. He read the book by accident, drawn at first to the title and then realising that he recognised the author. He reviewed the book for *Vanity Fair* and signed the review 'Oliver Haddo'. He made much of the thoughts, attitudes, philosophies, incidents, doctrines and personal mythology that had been lifted from his life and accused Maugham of a form of plagiarism. Nevertheless, Crowley revelled in the attention.

Maugham was on the cusp of immense popularity, a few years away from writing his defining novel *Of Human Bondage*. Maugham's wealth and distinction would rise in proportion to the diminishing of Crowley's fortunes. Crowley and Maugham would not meet again, but Crowley would later send Maugham a begging letter asking for £25. Maugham ignored the letter.

MATHERS, ROSE & AIWASS

In 1902 Crowley's reunion with Mathers in Paris resulted in a falling-out more acrimonious than their mutual rift with The Hermetic Order. While they both had a common enemy, Crowley and Mathers made reasonably good allies, but given both men's monumental egos and their antipathy to sharing power, a clash was inevitable. According to Crowley's version of events, the promised magical duel that never materialised between Mathers, Crowley and the London members of the Order erupted in Paris between the teacher and his former pupil. Crowley would claim that Mathers sent a succubus to drain and kill him in the form of an obese lady who transformed herself into a beautiful vampiric creature.

In 1903 the great hedonist married. He wedded his friend Gerald Kelley's sister Rose. He did it to liberate her from an unwanted engagement. Crowley and Rose's attitude to the marriage was initially frivolous. The couple, nevertheless, consummated the union and for a while found that they actually quite liked one another, deciding to live as man and wife. They went on a tour of France, North Africa and Ceylon. Rose fell pregnant and the couple made plans to return to Bolskein. In 1904, as they stopped off in Egypt, Crowley claimed an experience that would colour everything in his life from that point onwards.

Using Rose as a conduit, something tried to contact Crowley. The magician believed the creature trying to communicate with him was the Egyptian god Horus. Rose informed her husband that the creature's name was Aiwass, an angelic being speaking on behalf of the Secret Chiefs. Aiwass via Rose persuaded Crowley to convert their current lodgings into a temple. Before long Crowley began to hear Aiwass' voice for himself, and between 8 and 10 April Aiwass dictated a series of teachings that Crowley duly transcribed. The central concept of the teachings was the doctrine of Theluma, a Greek word meaning 'will'. The philosophy of Theluma was as intricate as the complex beliefs of the Order of the Golden Dawn, but was encapsulated in the statement: 'Do What Thou Willt shall be the whole of the law.' Theluma was essentially a new religion and Crowley had been appointed its prophet. In time, Theluma would be more colloquially known as Crowleyanity.

THE WICKEDEST MAN IN THE WORLD

In 1905 Rose gave birth to a daughter named Nuit Ma Ahathoor Hecate Sappho Jezebel Lilith. Later that year Crowley was part of an exhibition to climb Kanchenjunga. He fell out with the entire team and set up his own camp significantly apart from, but still within earshot of, the rest of the climbers. Then there was an accident. Two coolies and two climbers fell down the side of the mountain triggering an avalanche. Crowley could hear the stricken party's pleas for assistance; he had the skill to help them and was in a position to do so but he chose to do nothing and wilfully kept himself to himself. Three people died. Crowley was despised for his cruelty and indifference, and shunned by the mountaineering community.

Crowley's travels continued. He was a negligent father and his marriage began to deteriorate. Rose was drinking heavily and Crowley was not even present when his daughter died of typhoid. He blamed Rose and divorced her shortly afterwards. A few years later she was institutionalised.

In 1907 Crowley returned to England. His reputation as a dark prophet of a decadent new religion had begun to blossom. He wrote a great deal and began to accumulate disciples. In 1909 Crowley established his own publication, *The Equinox*, in which he exposed various secrets of The Hermetic Order of the Golden Dawn and was sued for 'Breach of spiritual copyright'. He lost the case but won the appeal. The press began to show interest in him.

At Claxton Hall in London Crowley and various acolytes performed the Eleusinian Rites. Press interest increased as observers came to Claxton Hall in the hope that they would see something supernatural or sexual. Thrill seekers were invariably disappointed. Nothing that salacious or magical happened. Nevertheless, Crowley was now established as, at the very least, an eccentric presence in the capital. And although there were individuals, communities and societies that detested Crowley, he was not yet the universal hate figure he would shortly become.

When war broke out in 1914 Crowley left Britain for America. Ever the provocateur, he threw in with a group of influential Germans and began to write for an anti-British publication called *The Fatherland*. He edited his own similarly themed periodical *The International*. He renounced British citizenship and was highly vocal in his support of the Irish rebellion. Surprisingly, the British government wasn't overly concerned about Crowley's treasonable conduct, although they did request a New Scotland Yard report on his background and activities. When the war was over, Crowley returned to England with very little recrimination. The exception was the publication *John Bull*, which was explicit in its hatred of Crowley.

Crowley's years of profligacy had caught up with him. His adventures had drained his immense reserves of cash and he was broke. He was forced to sell Bolskein. He also began experimenting with opium and hashish. He was suffering from a dyspnoeic condition and had been legally prescribed heroine. It would not take long for Crowley to cultivate a serious drug habit. He acquired another lover in Lea Hirsing, who bore him a daughter named Anne Lea.

Crowley's next project was the setting up of an abbey where Theluma could be taught to willing disciples. Between 1920 and 1923, the Abbey of Theluma, making more impact than his anti-British salvos during the war and his conduct on the face of Kanchenjunga, would succeed in establishing Crowley's reputation as the most controversial Englishman of his generation. The irony was that the abbey, in its own bizarre way, was a perfectly sincere endeavour.

The location of the abbey was a one-storey house overlooking the town of Cefalù in northern Sicily. Crowley and Hirsing dressed the house to look more like a temple, hanging up many of Crowley's transgressive, blasphemous and pornographic paintings. Anyone was welcome at the abbey provided they could make the journey. They were obliged to pay 50 guineas for a three-month stay. Abbey routine consisted of recitations in the morning, at noon and night, physical work, as well as the practice of sexual magic, some of which (at least as practised by Crowley and Hirsing) was deeply sadomasochistic. Drugs were present. Hygiene was appalling.

Crowley funded much of the abbey out of his own pocket. In order to earn money he was obliged to write a novel and Collins published the semi-autobiographical *The Diary of a Drug Fiend*. He was paid a reasonable advance, with the promise of a further £120 up front for his memoirs. The novel managed to offend the *Sunday Express* newspaper, after which Collins capitulated to pressure from the paper and refused to print further copies. They also reneged on the memoir deal.

Crowley's personal life at the abbey was contentious and tragic. His daughter with Hirsing died. She conceived again but Crowley had also impregnated the nanny. There would be another death at the abbey, the ripple effect of which would permanently mark Crowley's reputation.

Crowley had gone to London to write *The Diary of a Drug Fiend*. When he returned to Sicily he brought two people with him. One was a promising young disciple named Frederick Charles Loveday. The other was Loveday's wife, Betty May. Loveday threw himself into abbey life. Betty May was suspicious of Crowley and had only really come to the abbey to protect her husband from Crowley's influence. Tensions between Betty May and Crowley were palpable from the beginning and erupted at one point into a physical confrontation. Hostilities reached an untenable point when Loveday died of gastroenteritis contracted from drinking dirty water taken from a stream on a hike.

For once Crowley was not to blame, having actually advised Loveday not to drink the water. In his own way he cared for Loveday and was visibly distraught when he died. Betty May returned to London. She gave an interview to the *Sunday Express* in which she claimed Loveday had died after drinking cat's blood in a sacrificial ritual. The *Sunday Express* pilloried Crowley. When they were done with him *John Bull* took up the slack and virtually accused Crowley of murdering Loveday. They didn't stop there. Unfounded claims of child molestation and cannibalism were also levelled at Crowley, and it was *John Bull* that first called Aleistair Crowley 'the wickedest man in the world'.

Although the die had been permanently cast in terms of the popular reputation of Crowley as an evil diabolist, the debacle of the Abbey of Theluma was the high watermark of notoriety during his lifetime. There were still moments of controversy, however. In 1929 his bad reputation was such that the police effectively expelled him from Paris. His relationship with Hirsing came to an end. There would be other significant romances: a marriage to the Venezuelan Teresa Ferrari de Miramar and a love affair with the German painter Hanni Jaeger. Crowley would continue to struggle with his drug addiction. His finances dwindled to virtually nothing. He would be declared bankrupt, banned from speaking at the Poetry Society of Oxford, permanently estranged from his eldest surviving daughter, sued for libel and would earn a criminal conviction for theft when he was found to have stolen some of Betty May Loveday's personal correspondence. In the middle of all this chaos he wrote the novel *Moonchild*, and eventually found a publisher who would put out his memoirs.

As the 1920s and '30s slipped by, the Wickedest Man in the World was forced into the role of English eccentric. He still had the power to fascinate, but amusement rather than fear tended to be the reaction of many that sought his company. Amongst those who met Crowley in London was a popular novelist with a rising reputation. He would set in stone the fictional template for how Crowley would be regarded from that point onwards. And once again London would be the imaginary backdrop to some of the action.

WHEATLEY & CROWLEY

In the 1930s Dennis Wheatley was a wealthy, politically conservative veteran of the Great War, who was on the way to becoming a formidable commercial force in the world of publishing. He had already written *The Forbidden Territory*, an adventure novel in which four resourceful friends tangle with Communists and rescue a princess in post-revolutionary Russia. Wheatley was quite taken with his heroic quartet. He loved the writing of Alexander Dumas and wanted to create a modern variation of Dumas' musketeers. *The Forbidden Territory* was a financial success and Wheatley wrote a sequel. The follow-up would pit Wheatley's heroes against a powerful order of Satanists and the strange monsters at their command. It was a bold and unorthodox move, akin to John Buchan, after writing *The 39 Steps*, suddenly deciding that he wanted his hero Richard Hannay to fight Dracula instead of a German spy ring for the sequel. It proved a shrewd decision. The novel was *The Devil Rides Out*, the chief Satanist a bold, overweight, highly educated gentleman with a penetrating stare.

Dennis Wheatley and Aleister Crowley were introduced to each other by a mutual friend, the politician Tom Drieberg. Drieberg was an unpleasant man who would later in life count among his associates the Kray Twins. He had formerly been a disciple of Crowley's but the balance of power had shifted. Crowley was now something of a parasite – he was broke and pestering Drieberg for money.

Wheatley was aware of Crowley's past reputation but Crowley was not a particularly threatening presence at the time of their meeting. Wheatley considered the magician a fascinating and intelligent eccentric. They dined together; they exchanged books; they found common ground in ultra-conservative politics and a mutual love of Charles II. Crowley tried to engage Wheatley in a magical rite but Wheatley declined. The acquaintance didn't last very long and the two men drifted out of each other's orbit. In all probability, Wheatley tired of Crowley and deflected the magician's attempts to extend the friendship. But the possibilities of another exaggerated, fictional version of the man were irresistible.

MOCATA & *THE DEVIL RIDES OUT*

As in Somerset Maugham's *The Magician*, *The Devil Rides Out* is about the fight by a devoted band of friends for the imperilled soul of one of their number. Wheatley's heroes are the exiled French aristocrat the Duc de Richelieu; Rex Van Ryan, a brawny American action man; Richard Eaton, an excellent pilot married to a Russian princess; and Simon Arum, a sensitive, thoughtful, slightly built Jew. Simon Arum has fallen under the influence of a band of Satanists led by the powerful Mocata. The satanic order wishes to re-baptise Arum on Saint Worthington's Eve: a ceremony that will irretrievably damn his soul to hell. Richelieu and company attempt to rescue Arum. After a few botched attempts they succeed, but the battle isn't over. They must now protect their friend from an array of demonic attacks as Mocata dispatches sundry creatures to reclaim him.

London features prominently in the early chapters of *The Devil Rides Out*. The action oscillates between Simon Arum's large house in St John's Wood, with its own observatory and occult mosaics, and Richelieu's fashionable Curzon Street apartment. There is an encounter with a witch at Claridge's, and the British Museum doubles as an occult armoury in which Richelieu accumulates the esoteric knowledge needed to battle Mocata.

Unlike the London of Maugham's *The Magician*, where nothing supernatural ever really happens, Wheatley's capital city uses its respectable locations as a glossy veneer behind which malevolent paranormal activity takes place. The first of *The Devil Rides Out*'s many supernatural clashes takes place in Arum's St John's Wood residence, where Van Ryan and Richelieu are almost

Mocata. (Illustrated by Jean Nightingale)

bested by a demon that takes the form of a large black servant of Mocata's. Eventually, the action moves from London to Salisbury Plain, Stonehenge, Richard Eaton's Kidderminster home, Paris, and finally, a ruined abbey in Greece.

The Devil Rides Out is a bad novel on many levels, a horror *Boy's Own* adventure. Each chapter ends on a melodramatic cliffhanger. With one notable exception, Wheatley's characters are stock cardboard heroes and villains. Wheatley employs a simple physical shorthand to demonstrate who is good and who is bad. In Wheatley's universe, if you are handsome you are probably good. The uglier you are, the more evil you are likely to be. God help you if you are black (*The Devil Rides Out* is casually, appallingly and often comically racist in places).

Wheatley never made any great claims as an artist. He was quite outspoken in his belief that his only obligation as a writer was to tell a good story. This would be fair enough if much of *The Devil Rides Out* weren't so boring. Wheatley the researcher seems constantly at odds with Wheatley the entertainer. He had clearly done extensive background reading (much of it no doubt provided by Crowley), but he had a pathological need to let the reader know at every opportunity exactly how much homework he had done. So, just when the novel looks like it might explode into life, it often judders to a halt for a long and pedantic lecture on some avenue of occult knowledge or witchcraft history.

Wheatley is good at terrain, architecture and monsters. His descriptions of old buildings and ancient landscapes, where something timeless and evil is resident, are terse, economic and ominous. And if *The Devil Rides Out* deserves its continued place on the bookshelves, it is because of its vivid bestiary of creatures at Mocata's beck and call. The numerous confrontations between Wheatley's heroes and Mocata's 'Ab-Human monsters' are atmospheric and dramatic. The celebrated sequence in which Richard Eaton's house is besieged for one endless evening by living shadows, rapid changes in temperature, howling winds, counterfeit voices, apparitions, a slug-like demon and finally the Angel of Death itself, deserves its reputation for expertly written cumulative horror.

If humans didn't particularly interest Wheatley, then there was one exception. Mocata stands out among the cardboard characters. This is not to say that Mocata is a complex creation; he is pure evil. Of the three fictional black magicians featured in this chapter, Mocata is by far the nastiest, at one point attempting to sacrifice Richard Eaton's young daughter. He is more powerful than Haddo or Karswell. The creatures at his disposal are greater than anything summoned or created by Karswell or Haddo. Mocata is more megalomaniacal and nihilistic. As the narrative progresses, we discover that

Mocata's interest is Simon Arum is rooted in the fact that buried in his subconscious is the location of an Egyptian artefact that has the power to release the Four Horsemen of the Apocalypse, and immerse the world in warfare and bloodshed.[1]

Like Karswell in *Casting the Runes*, Mocata is eventually destroyed by one of the creatures he has invoked. Like Karswell, Mocata is kept off the page for much of the narrative: his movements are reported; he is seen in the distance; his acolytes and victims talk of his incredible power, and his power is felt in the numerous beasts he sends to reclaim Simon Arum. But Mocata only really has one scene in which he is directly the centre of attention. In Chapter 22 Mocata ingratiates himself into the home of Richard Eaton. He encounters Eaton's wife, Marie Lou. She is naturally wary of him. Mocata begins a lengthy justification of his belief system. What at first appears to be another Wheatley lecture making another unwelcome appearance actually justifies its inclusion in narrative terms as the reader becomes aware that Mocata is hypnotising and seducing Marie Lou. The longer Mocata speaks, the more Marie Lou comes under his influence. The spell is broken when Marie Lou's daughter enters the room. Mocata leaves and doesn't appear again until the novel's climax. The encounter between Mocata and Marie Lou has a subtlety lacking in any other human exchange in the novel, leaving Mocata the most delicately drawn character in *The Devil Rides Out*. And although Wheatley makes Mocata half-Irish, half-French, gives him a lisp and a past as a defrocked priest, there is much of the real Aleister Crowley in Mocata: his physical appearance, his intellect, his eyes, and his ability (in spite of everything traditionally repellent about him) to attract women.

The Devil Rides Out was an astronomical success. Wheatley's name would become synonymous with the black magic subgenre of horror (despite only writing seven or so horror titles out of a total of seventy novels). The Duc and his friends would appear in other adventures but these are not generally read today. *The Devil Rides Out* is still in print, and although not the best-written vehicle for a fictional version of Crowley, it remains today the best remembered.[2]

OTHER CROWLEYS

Karswell, Haddo and Mocata were the tip of the iceberg. Fictional versions of Crowley have been legion ever since and fascination with the magician shows no sign of dying out. In the pantheon of literary fiction and horror literature, it is doubtful that any other equivalent historical figure has been regurgitated as often as Aleister Crowley: the Christian novelist (and former member of

The Hermetic Order of the Golden Dawn) Charles Williams contributed what is commonly believed to be a version of Crowley in the supernatural thriller *All Hallows' Eve*. The running nemesis of John Thunston, the recurring hero of American horror-writer Manley Wade Wellman, was based on Crowley. Anthony Powell actually met Crowley and used him as the basis for two characters in his mammoth work *The Dance to the Music of Time*. A walk-on appearance by the real Aleister Crowley is the punch line to a chapter in *A Moveable Feast*, Ernest Hemingway's account of his time as a young writer in Paris. Christopher Isherwood wrote a character inspired by Crowley in *A Visit to Anselm Oaks*. Ian Fleming drew on his encounters with Crowley for 'Le Chiffre', James Bond's first and most sadistic adversary. Graphic novelist Alan Moore revived Oliver Haddo as one of *The League of Extraordinary Gentlemen*'s enemies. As King Lemus, Crowley even contributed a highly idealised self-portrait in *The Diary of a Drug Fiend*.

The Cult of Crowley re-emerged in the 1960s and he became a poster boy for all things occult. He was one of the faces on the Beatles' 'Sgt Pepper' album cover, Ozzy Osbourne sang about him and Led Zeppelin guitarist Jimmy Page bought his old house, Bolskein. The need to provide thinly disguised fictional versions of Crowley gave way to Crowley himself appearing in works of fiction. The novelist, critic and horror historian Kim Newman used him as the villain in his short story *Angel Down Sussex*. In *Heaven's War*, graphic novelist Micah Harris imagined a metaphysical conflict between Crowley and the Christian triumvirate of writers, Charles Williams, C.S. Lewis and J.R.R. Tolkien. Iron Maiden frontman Bruce Dickinson wrote and directed the horror film *Chemical Wedding* with Simon Callow as Crowley. More recently, Jake Arnott's novel, *The Devil's Paintbrush*, elaborated the real-life relationship between the young Aleister Crowley and the disgraced Victorian soldier, Major-General Sir Hector Macdonald. There are many more examples.

Crowley would no doubt have been thrilled with his fictional legacy. He would have considered it his due right. But Crowley's death was more ignominious than he would have planned. In December 1947 Aleister Crowley died in a Hastings boarding house of natural causes. There are a number of versions of how he met his end. The kindest has him dying in peace in a cheerful mood, his passing accompanied by the wind disturbing the curtains and a roll of thunder. Harsher accounts have him weeping, his final words being, 'I am perplexed' and 'Sometimes I hate myself'.

NOTES

2. The Great Feud: In Print

1 Jonathan Wild had one final ironic part to play in Henry Fielding's life. Henry and his brother John formed the Bow Street Runners, a highly effective proto police force that brought a greater degree of protection and stability to the London streets than had been previously known. In organising the runners, the Fielding brothers adapted many of Wild's administrative ideas, turned them on their head and made them work successfully for the purposes of law enforcement.

2 There is a school of thought that points to an implicit criticism present in Hogarth's illustrations of Goodchild's arguably Machiavellian rout to respectability, as well as a belief that Hogarth sees Tom Idle's fate, in spite of his fatal choices, as being as much predetermined by environment than anything else.

3 Drawing on the examples of all the great writers that had gone before them, Ainsworth and Doyle seemed to establish between them the beginnings of the ground rules for what a classic master villain should be. Both villains had exotic henchmen (Wild's Abraham Mendez and Moriarty's right-hand man Colonel Sebastian Moran) and a small criminal army that enforced and administered a complex secret empire. Ainsworth's villain had his own fortified lair and a penchant for explaining his plans to his enemies before attempting to kill them in elaborate ways, permitting them the opportunity to escape and thwart the plans that he had just revealed to them. These are qualities that would be embraced in the twentieth century by James Bond's various nemeses, as Ian Fleming's series of spy novels and the films that followed became the template by which master villainy would be understood and subsequently parodied.

4 In 1969 *Where's Jack?*, a feature film about Sheppard and Wild, was directed
by the Shogun novelist James Clavell. It starred the pop singer Tommy Steele
as Jack Sheppard, while Wild was played by Stanley Baker (who also produced
the film). Neither of them were strictly obvious custodians of the Sheppard/
Wild legacy. Baker's involvement made more sense. Although the popular
memory of him now is dominated by his performance as Lieutenant Chard
in the colonial war epic *Zulu*, Baker was one of the key figures in the evolution of British crime cinema. Pre-empting the iconographic dominance of
actors such as Michael Caine and Bob Hoskins, in tough dramas such as *The
Criminal*, *Hell Drivers* and *Hell is a City*, Baker had brought new layers of
violence, sexuality and rebellious class-discord to the hoodlums, drifters and
police officers of 1950s and '60s British cinema. In his personal life he seemed
to hold two worlds in tension. He was devoted to his family, was a social-
ist who never forgot his Welsh working-class roots, and was a scrupulously
fair businessman. Yet he kept company with and counted among his friends
London mobsters such as Albert Dimes and the Richardson Gang's violent
enforcer, "Mad" Frankie Fraser.

Prior to *Where's Jack?*, Baker, as producer and actor, had scored one of his
biggest commercial successes with *Robbery*. After *Robbery* his production
company would have a hand in making the quintessential swinging sixties
crime caper *The Italian Job*. *Robbery* was a forensic recreation of the Great
Train Robbery, with Baker playing a barely fictionalised version of British
criminal Bruce Reynolds. *The Italian Job* was pure comic fantasy, Ealing
comedy as filtered through a '60s prism of dolly birds, mini coopers, Noel
Coward, Benny Hill, Michael Caine, patriotism and Quincy Jones' wonderful
Rule Britannia jazz.

Where's Jack? was sandwiched between these polar opposite representations
of British criminality. It was filmed in Ireland and managed to recreate the
hustle, filth and excitement of Georgian London and tavern life very well.
The natural set pieces from the Wild/Sheppard story are present. Their feud
is seen in terms of rebellious independent free spirit versus a perverted version of the establishment as represented by Wild and his organisation. Wild
and Sheppard, although natural opponents, are less antagonistic in this version
of their story. Wild even sees something of an alternate path he might have
taken in the example of Sheppard. It doesn't stop Wild hanging Sheppard,
however. But the final sound the audience hear is that of heavy breathing as
Jack's body, cut down from Tyburn Tree and whisked away by friends, slowly
revives in the narrative tradition that dictates that Sheppard cannot be allowed
to die. *Where's Jack?* was as commercially unsuccessful as the two films that
bookended it were popular. It is hardly screened these days, barely remembered and at the time of writing unavailable on DVD.

3. A Notorious Baggage

1 Although not a London work, Thomas Middleton had written one of the few Jacobean tragedies to draw on contemporary crime. *The Yorkshire Tragedy* (1606) is a short work inspired by the crimes of Walter Calverley, who in 1605 murdered his two sons and attempted to kill his wife when intimations about his children's legitimacy were raised. Calverley would neither plead guilty nor not guilty. He was pressed to death, the awful legal consequence of refusing to plea.

2 Dekker and Shakespeare were both thought to have been amongst the numerous collaborators for the Lord Chamberlain's Men on the play *Sir Thomas More*.

4. Two 'Spectable Old Gentlemen

1 Dickens never overtly calls Nancy a prostitute but heavily infers such a profession when towards the end of *Oliver Twist*, Nancy describes herself as follows: "'Thank Heaven upon your knees, dear lady ... that you had friends to care for and keep you in your childhood, and that you were never in the midst of cold and hunger, and riot and drunkenness, and—and—something worse than all—as I have been from my cradle.'"

2 In 1840 Dickens attended the execution of Francois Courvoisier, a Swiss valet who murdered his master. In 1849 Dickens was present at the double hanging of Frederick and Maria Manning. The Mannings were also murderers. With her husband's consent, Maria Manning had seduced a man named Patrick O'Connor and killed him for his money. Dickens wrote an account of the hanging for *The Times* newspaper. His focus was the appalling vice on display in the crowd for whom public execution was supposed to act as a deterrent, rather than the execution itself. Maria Manning would become the inspiration for the character of Hortense in *Bleak House*.

3 Dickens documented his journey through the rookery of St Giles with the famous police officer in *On Duty With Inspector Field*, believed by many to be one of the best pieces of journalism Dickens ever wrote. A fictional version of Field appears in *Bleak House* in the form of Inspector Bucket.

4 A case is often made by Dickens scholars that Sikes and Nancy contributed to his death at the age of 58. Nancy's murder became the centrepiece of a series of public readings Dickens performed towards the end of his life. The intensity of the readings frightened audiences and caused questions to once again be raised about the innate appropriateness of the sequence. Dickens would throw himself into the recreation of the murder. It exacted a huge toll physically and he died of a heart attack. The readings are thought by many to have contributed towards the heart attack.

5. The Man Who Killed Sherlock Holmes

1   When playing Sherlock Holmes, Gillette elected to wear a deerstalker hat, contributing the most recognisable element to Holmes' visual iconography.

2   Presumably to prevent accusations of monumental callousness and insensitivity being laid at the feet of Holmes, Doyle has his detective explain to Watson that had he revealed himself to his dearest friend at any point during the previous three years, he would have risked exposure to his enemies.

3   *The Illustrious Client* contains a reference to a real-life master criminal. Holmes states early on in the story: 'A complex mind ... All great criminals have that. My old friend Charlie Peace was a violin virtuoso.' Charles Peace was an expert burglar and double murderer. He was a master of disguise, athletic, and a gifted violinist. He was violent and paranoid but also one of the great criminal eccentrics of the Victorian age. He was subject to one of the most famous manhunts in nineteenth-century England. If he hadn't already existed, Doyle would no doubt have invented him.

4   The fact that 221b Baker Street was burned under Moriarty's orders is all but glossed over in *The Empty House*.

6. Little Adam & The Eye

1   One of the Pinkertons' great successes had been the demolition of the politicised criminal organisation, the Molly Maguires. The case had been written up by Alan Pinkerton and published. Doyle plundered the account for the majority of *The Valley of Fear*'s American plot. Pinkerton interpreted this as an act of virtual plagiarism. The result was a rift between Doyle and Pinkerton.

7. Feasting With Panthers

1   The rift birthed a casually racist denunciation of Hornung where Doyle expressed discomfort at the friendship when he considered the 'fact that William is half Mongol half Slav, or whatever the mixture is'.

2   In *Nine Points of the Law*, Raffles is employed to steal back an expensive, stolen Velasquez painting and return it to its owner. The new owner of the painting is in one room while the painting is concealed in another. Raffles arranges a meeting between Bunny and the current owner of the stolen work of art at his apartment. Raffles intends to break into the apartment while Bunny is distracting the owner. He substitutes the real painting for an impeccable forgery but neglects to tell Bunny. Bunny takes the chance to observe the painting for himself. He sees the forgery not realising it is a fake. He thinks Raffles has botched the theft. Bunny returns to the apartment later that evening and steals the forgery believing it to be the real Velasquez.

3   The Albany must be one of the most famous literary addresses in London's West End. In addition to its place in the Raffles geography, the Albany is used by Oscar Wilde in *The Importance of Being Earnest* as Jack Worthing's London address.

8. The Wickedest Man in the World

1   Why Mocata wants to do this is unclear; but of two of the more inadvertently comical asides in *The Devil Rides Out*, the first is the realisation that this has been done once before by none other than Rasputin and the consequence was the First World War. The second is that the artefact that triggers the Apocalypse is called the Talisman of Set and turns out to be an Egyptian god's penis.

2   The enduring popularity of *The Devil Rides Out* probably has as much to do with the superb 1968 Hammer Studio film adaptation as the novel itself. In fact, the film is that rare movie animal that improves on its source material. Although elegantly directed by Terrence Fisher and featuring a strong central performance by Christopher Lee as Richelieu, most of the credit must go to the screenwriter Richard Matheson (a horror and science fiction writer of great distinction). It is Matheson that streamlines Wheatley's narrative and removes most of his appalling dialogue. There is more of Mocata and he is given lines to speak that you wish were in the novel. As played by Charles Grey, Mocata is one of cinema's great horror villains (Grey also contributed the best Blofeld in the James Bond series and played Sherlock Holmes' brother Mycroft in the long-running ITV series starring Jeremy Brett). But there is little or nothing of Crowley in Grey's Mocata. In fact, the suave Satanist seems more modelled on Dennis Wheatley than Aleister Crowley.